• TROPHIES •

English-Language Learners Copying Masters

Grade 1

Harcourt

Orlando   Boston   Dallas   Chicago   San Diego

Visit *The Learning Site!*
www.harcourtschool.com

Printed in the United States of America

ISBN 0-15-325057-7

4 5 6 7 8 9 10 022 10 09 08 07 06 05 04 03

Contents

Contents

HERE AND THERE – LEVEL 3

TIME TOGETHER – LEVEL 4

Contents

TIME TOGETHER – LEVEL 4

GATHER AROUND – LEVEL 5

· TROPHIES ·

Level One

Guess Who

Name _____

▶ **Say the name of each picture. The name of each circled picture has the /a/ sound. Color the circled pictures.**

1.

pig

2.

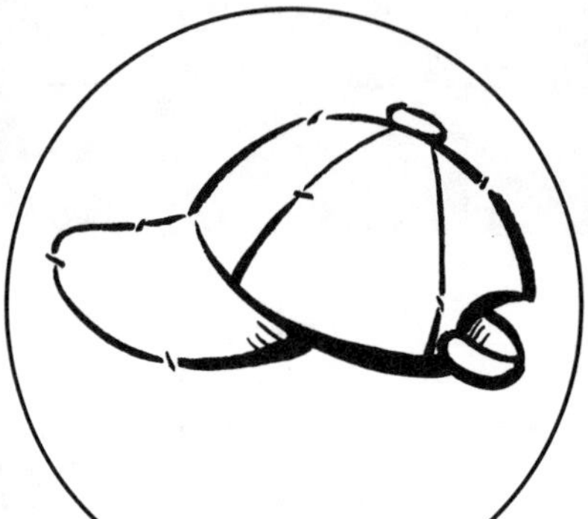

cap

3.

leg

4.

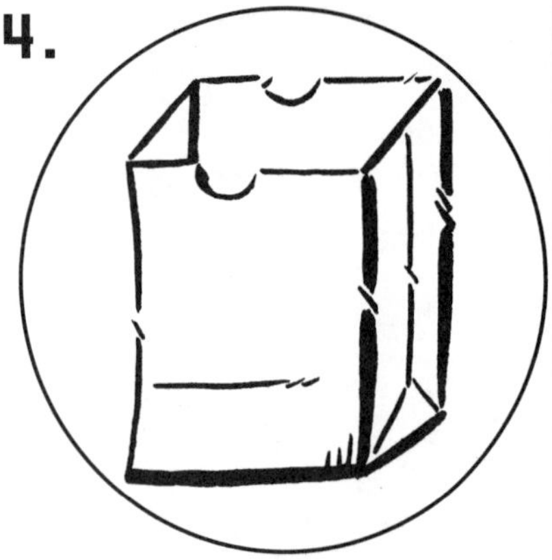

bag

5.

web

6.

cup

7.

ham

8.

pen

9.

cat

For the Teacher With children, identify each picture. Stretch the short *a* sound as you say the name of each picture name with short *a*. Have children repeat each word.

English-Language Learners
Guess Who • Lesson 1

▶ **One picture in each set has the vowel sound /a/ as in <u>at</u>. That picture is circled. Color the circled picture, and say its name.**

1.
 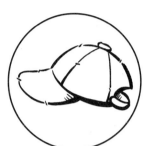

2.

3.

4.

5.
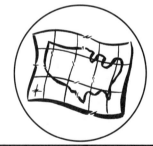 

6.

7.

8.

For the Teacher Emphasize vowel sounds as you identify the pictures. Have children repeat each picture name. Draw a circle on the chalkboard, and remind children to color only the pictures in the circles.

11

English-Language Learners
Guess Who • Lesson 1

► **Look at each picture and read the sentence. Cut out the word that completes the sentence. Paste the word in the sentence.**

1. I look [   ].

2. I look [   ].

3. I [   ] on!

✂

| up | down | got |

For the Teacher Talk about the words at the bottom of the page. Read each word aloud, and have children repeat it. Read each sentence with children, guiding them in understanding the words.

English-Language Learners
Guess Who • Lesson 1

Name _____

▶ **Look at each picture. Cut out the word that completes the sentence. Paste the word in the sentence.**

1.

cat

I am a [_____].

2.

mat

I have a [_____].

3.

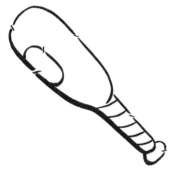

bat

I have a [_____].

4.

cap

I have a [_____].

- -
| **cat** | **cap** | **mat** | **bat** |
- -

For the Teacher Discuss each picture. Say the picture name, and have children repeat it. Point to the word *cat* at the bottom of the page. Explain that children should cut out the box with the word *cat*. Show children where to paste it. Guide children in completing the page.

13

English-Language Learners
Guess Who • Lesson 1

Name _____

▶ **Write 1, 2, and 3 to put the pictures in order.**

_____

_____

_____

_____

_____

_____

For the Teacher Discuss each set of pictures with children.
Invite volunteers to tell what is happening in each picture.
Then have children number the pictures in each set.

14

English-Language Learners
Guess Who • Lesson 1

Name _____

▶ **Name each picture. Draw a line between words that rhyme.**

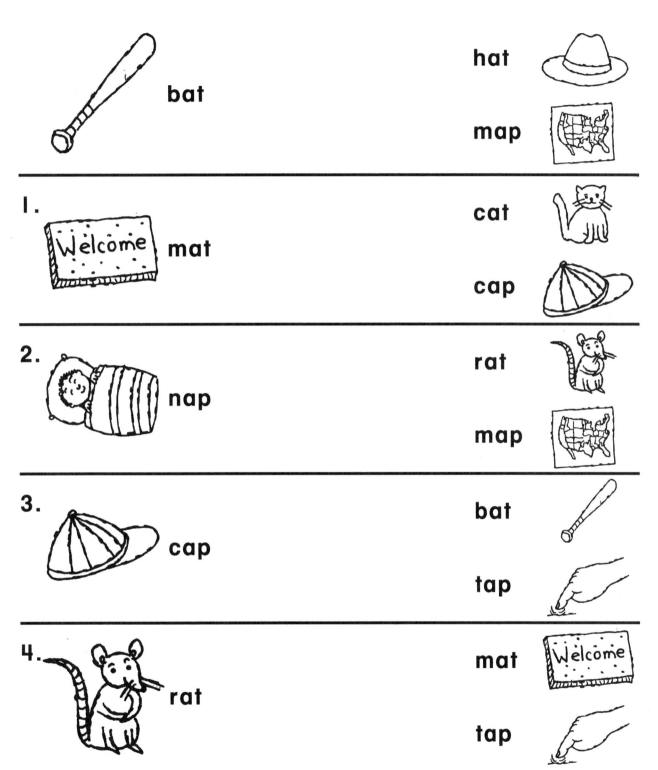

bat   hat

                       map

1. mat   cat

                       cap

2. nap   rat

                       map

3. cap   bat

                       tap

4. rat   mat

                       tap

For the Teacher With children, identify the pictures, stressing the final sound of each picture name. Work through the sample with children. Show them how to draw a line to the matching word.

15

English-Language Learners
Guess Who • Lesson 1

Name _____

▶ **Say the name of the first picture in each row. Color the picture in the row whose name rhymes with it.**

1.

fan

cat

pan

2.

cap

map

nest

3.

ham

ten

jam

4.

hat

bike

bat

For the Teacher Identify each picture. Explain to children that the rhyming words on this page have the short *a* sound as in *at*.

17

English-Language Learners
Guess Who • Lesson 2

Name _____

▶ **Look at the pictures and the words. Color each picture whose name has the vowel sound /a/ as in <u>at</u>.**

1.

map

2.

can

3.

nest

4.

bib

5.

bat

6.

cap

7.

pig

8.

cat

For the Teacher Be certain that children can identify the pictures. Before children begin to color, talk about which words have the short *a* sound.

English-Language Learners
Guess Who • Lesson 2

Name _____

▶ **Look at each picture and read the sentence. Trace the word that completes the sentence.**

1. Jan  Max ran.

2. Jan ran  the cap.

3. Can Max go  ?

4.  , Max can.

5.  , Max!

For the Teacher Read aloud the instructions. With children, read each sentence and talk about what is happening in the picture.

20

English-Language Learners
Guess Who • Lesson 2

Name _____

▶ **Look at each picture and read the sentence. Write the word.**

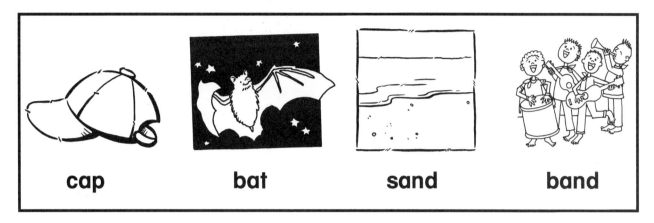

| cap | bat | sand | band |

1. This is a _____ .

_____

- - - - - - - - - - - - - - -

2. The hat is in the _____ .

_____

- - - - - - - - - - - - - - -

3. This is a _____ .

_____

- - - - - - - - - - - - - - -

4. The bat is in a _____ .

_____

- - - - - - - - - - - - - - -

For the Teacher Identify each picture. With children, read aloud each sentence. Talk about the word that makes sense to complete each sentence.

21

English-Language Learners
Guess Who • Lesson 2

▶ **Finish each sentence. Add s to the word above the line. Write the new word on the line.**

look

_____

- -

1. Pam _____.

pat

_____

- - - - - - - - - - - - - - - - - - - -

2. Sam _____ a cat.

come

_____

- -

3. The cat _____.

For the Teacher Read aloud the directions. With children, read each sentence and talk about what is happening in the picture. Have children complete the sentences.

22

English-Language Learners
Guess Who • Lesson 2

Name _____

▶ **Say the name of each picture. The name of each picture in a circle has the short i̱ sound. Color the circled pictures.**

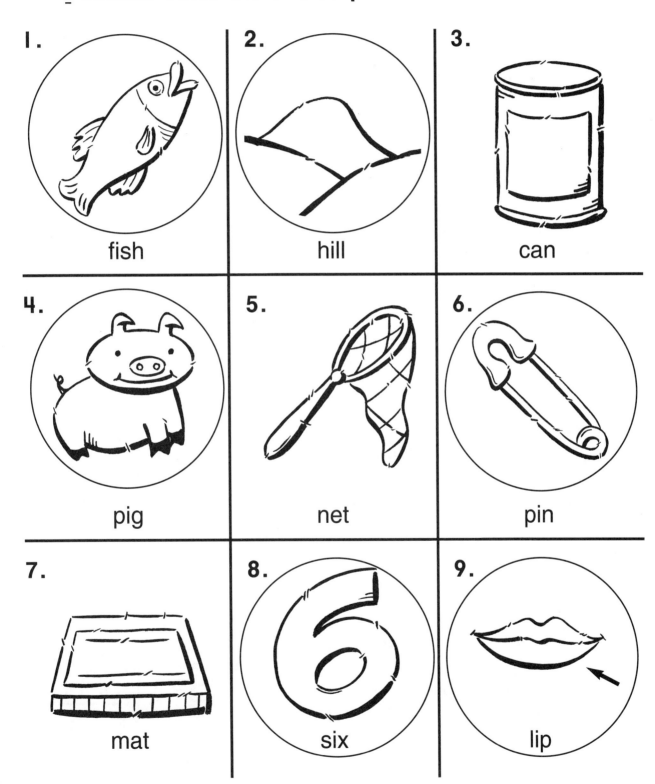

1. fish

2. hill

3. can

4. pig

5. net

6. pin

7. mat

8. six

9. lip

For the Teacher With children, identify each picture. Say each picture name aloud, emphasizing the short i sound in circled items. Have children echo each picture name.

24

English-Language Learners
Guess Who • Lesson 3

Name _____

▶ **Each picture that is circled has the vowel sound /i/ as in <u>it</u>. Color the circled pictures.**

1.

2.

3.

4.

5.

6.

 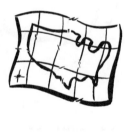

7.

8.

For the Teacher Stretch the vowel sound as you say each picture name. Have children repeat the picture names. Draw a circle on the chalkboard. Remind children to color only those pictures inside circles.

26

English-Language Learners
Guess Who • Lesson 3

Name _____

▶ **Cut out the words. Paste each word in the sentence where it belongs. Read the sentence.**

1. Kim and Jim can [_____] here.

2. [_____] walk in.

3. Kim and Jim [_____] a map.

✂ -

| **walk** | **They** | **make** |

For the Teacher Read the directions aloud. With children, read each sentence and the words at the bottom of the page. Demonstrate the meanings of words they do not understand. Guide children through the first item to be sure they understand the task.

27

English-Language Learners
Guess Who • Lesson 3

Name _____

▶ **Say the name of each picture. Trace the picture name. Each word has the sound /i/.**

1.

pig

2.

bib

3.

wig

4.

hill

5.

mitt

For the Teacher With children, identify each picture. Stretch the sound /i/, as you say each word and have children echo it. Show children how to trace the letters of the first word. Then have them complete the page and read the words aloud to a partner.

28

English-Language Learners
Guess Who • Lesson 3

Name _____

▶ **Look at the top picture. Then cut out the pictures in the small squares. Paste the smaller pictures where they belong in the bottom picture.**

For the Teacher With children, note the details in the top picture. Have children tell you where they see the ball, the bird, and the fish. Have children cut out the squares. Tell them to use the top picture to know where to paste the pictures in the bottom picture.

29

English-Language Learners
Guess Who • Lesson 3

▶ **Trace the contraction that completes each sentence.**

1.

Van is

Van's here.

2.

It is

It's a big cat.

3.

That is

That's for the cat.

For the Teacher With children, read each sentence aloud two times—the first time reading the two words and the second time reading the contraction. Point out the 's in each contraction.

English-Language Learners
Guess Who • Lesson 3

Name _____

▶ **Each circled picture on the backpack has the sound /k/ at the end. Color each circled picture.**

tack

sick

sack

hat

kick

tub

For The Teacher With children, identify each picture and read its name. Talk about which words have the /k/ sound at the end. Tell children that only the words in circles have /k/ at the end. Read the instructions, and remind children to color only the circled pictures.

32

English-Language Learners
Guess Who • Lesson 4

Name _____

▶ **Look at each picture and the picture name. Color the picture whose name ends with the sound /k/.**

1.

tack   pan

2.

Rick   bus

3.

dog   kick

For The Teacher With children, identify each picture and its name. Help children recognize each word that has the sound /k/ at the end. Read aloud the instructions, making certain that children understand the task.

34

English-Language Learners
Guess Who • Lesson 4

Name _____

▶ **Look at each picture and read the sentence. Cut out the word that completes the sentence. Paste the word in the sentence.**

1. Do you ⬚ to go?

2. I am ⬚ little.

3. I can ⬚ .

4. ⬚ I can go.

5. We can ⬚ .

want	too	help	Now	play

For The Teacher Read aloud the directions. With children, read aloud the first sentence. Guide children to cut out and paste *want* in the sentence. Then have them complete the page.

English-Language Learners
Guess Who • Lesson 4

Name _____

▶ **Circle the picture in each row whose name ends with the sound /k/, as in <u>sack</u>.**

1.

2.

3.

For The Teacher Say *sack*. Emphasize the sound /k/. Have children repeat. Read the directions to children. Identify each picture, making certain that children can recognize pictures whose names end in /k/ck. Remind children to circle only those pictures whose names end with the sound /k/.

36

English-Language Learners
Guess Who • Lesson 4

Name _____

▶ **Write 1, 2, and 3 to put the pictures in order.**

1.

_____   _____   _____

- - - - - - -   - - - - - - -   - - - - - - -

_____   _____   _____

2.

_____   _____   _____

- - - - - - -   - - - - - - -   - - - - - - -

_____   _____   _____

For The Teacher Talk with children about each set of
pictures. Have volunteers tell what is happening in each
set and identify what happens first, next and last. Then
have children number the pictures in each set.

37

English-Language Learners
Guess Who • Lesson 4

Name _____

▶ **Look at the two words above the sentence. Then circle the contraction that finishes each sentence.**

I will

1. I'll look up.

You will

2. You'll look down.

We will

3. We'll look in the bag.

For The Teacher Write I *will* on the chalkboard. Then write *I'll* below *I will*. Tell children that *I'll* is a contraction for the words *I will*. Show how an apostrophe (') is used in place of the letters *wi*. Circle *I'll* on the chalkboard. Explain that children should circle the contraction in each sentence.

English-Language Learners
Guess Who • Lesson 4

Name _____

▶ **Say the name of each picture. Each circled picture has the sound /o/. Color the circled pictures.**

1.

2.

3.

4.

5.

6.

7.

8.
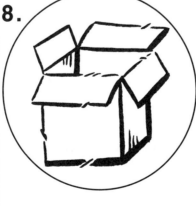

9.

For the Teacher With children, identify each picture. Stretch /o/ as you say *dog*. Have children repeat after you. Make certain that children can distinguish between words with and without the sound /o/. Remind children to color only those pictures whose names have the sound /o/.

English-Language Learners
Guess Who • Lesson 5

▶ **Color the pictures whose names have the vowel sound /o/.**

For the Teacher Stretch /o/ as you say *box*. Have children echo. With children, identify each picture. Remind children to color only pictures whose names have the vowel sound /o/.

42

English-Language Learners
Guess Who • Lesson 5

Name _____

▶ **Read the sentences. Trace the word that completes each sentence.**

1. The cat is **so** little.

2. The cat is on the back

 **of** the mitt.

3. Oh! **Don't** back up.

43

English-Language Learners
Guess Who • Lesson 5

Name _____

▶ **Cut out the pictures. If the picture's name has the short i sound, paste it below the pig. If it has the short o sound, paste it below the top.**

✂

For the Teacher Stretch /i/ as you say *pig*. Have children repeat the word. Repeat with /o/ in *top*. With children, identify each picture on the page, and read the directions. Discuss the short vowel sound in each word. Have children cut out the pictures and place them below the pig or top without pasting. Check children's work before they begin to paste.

44

Name _____

▶ **Look at the word and its ending. Then trace the new word that finishes each sentence.**

look + ed

1. The pig _looked_ at the bat.

look + ing

2. Pat is _looking_ at the pig now.

call + ed

3. Pat _called_ to the pig.

call + ing

4. Now the pig is _calling_ to Pat.

For the Teacher Write *look + ed* on the chalkboard. Then write *looked* below *look + ed*. Tell children that the ending *–ed* has been added to the word *look* to make a new word—*looked*. With children, read the directions. Write *looked* on the chalkboard, and trace it.

45

English-Language Learners
Guess Who • Lesson 5

Name _____

▶ **Each word at the bottom of the page ends with <u>all</u>. Cut out the words. Paste them on the big ball.**

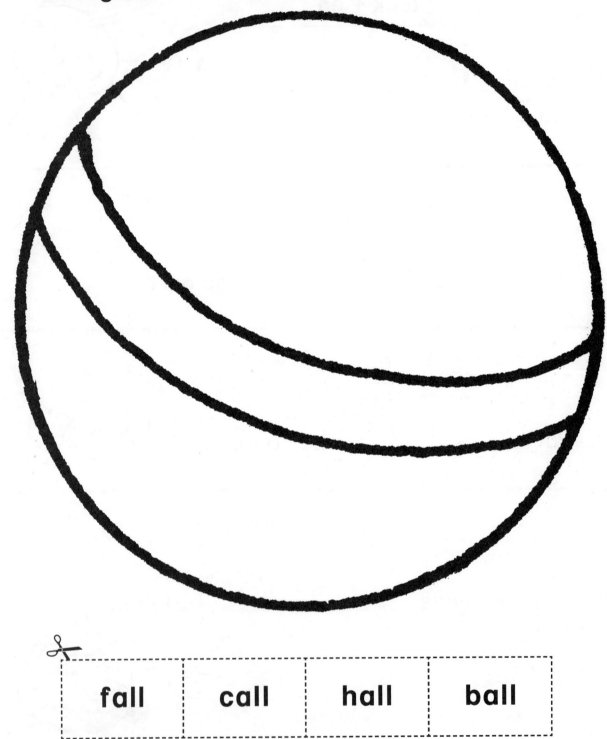

| fall | call | hall | ball |

For the Teachers Say *ball*. Point out that this word has sound /ô/ and ends with *all*. Read the directions with children. Then read each word aloud, pointing out the sound /ô/ and the *all* ending. Tell children to cut out each word and paste it on the big ball.

47

English-Language Learners
Guess Who • Lesson 6

Name _____

▶ **Circle each word that has <u>all</u>. Then trace the word.**

1. I have a ____ball____.

2. I ____call____ Max.

3. Now Max has ____all____ the balls.

For the Teachers Emphasize /ô/ as you say *call*, and have children repeat. Read the directions. Then read each sentence with children, making certain that children understand what they are to do. Encourage discussion about the pictures.

49

English-Language Learners
Guess Who • Lesson 6

Name _____

▶ **Read each sentence. Trace the word on the lines.**

1. _____ Where _____ is the ham?

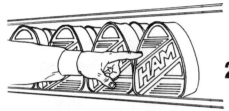

2. It is in _____ that _____ can.

3. It is a _____ very _____ big ham.

4. I will _____ buy _____ it.

For the Teachers Read the directions. Then read aloud
each sentence, and explain any words children
do not understand. Show children how to trace *Where*.

50

English-Language Learners
Guess Who • Lesson 6

Name _____

► **Read each sentence. Write the word that finishes the sentence.**

mitt	hill	hall	doll

1. I go up the _____.
   _____

2. The _____ is big.
   _____

3. My _____ is in a box.
   _____

4. We walk in the _____.
   _____

For the Teachers With children, discuss what is happening in each picture and read the sentence. Talk about the vowel sound in each word. Have children write the words.

English-Language Learners
Guess Who • Lesson 6

Name _____

▶ **Write 1, 2, and 3 to put the pictures in order.**

1.

_____   _____   _____

- - - - - -   - - - - - -   - - - - - -

2.

_____   _____   _____

- - - - - -   - - - - - -   - - - - - -

3.

_____   _____   _____

- - - - - -   - - - - - -   - - - - - -

For the Teachers Help children describe what is happening in each set of pictures, and ask volunteers to tell what happened first, next, and last. Then have children number the pictures in each set.

52

English-Language Learners
Guess Who • Lesson 6

▶ **Finish each sentence. Write the contraction for the two words above the lines.**

is + not

_____

- - - - - - - - - - - - - - - - -

1. The dog _____ here.

---

do + not

_____

- - - - - - - - - - - - - - - - -

2. I _____ see the dog.

---

are + not

_____

- - - - - - - - - - - - - - - - -

3. The cats _____ here.

Did + not

_____

- - - - - - - - - - - - - - - - -

4. _____ they come?

For the Teacher Read the directions. Then read each sentence, and talk about what is happening in the story. Write *is* and *not* on the chalkboard. Tell children that you will put the words together to make one new word. Write *isn't*. Remind children that an apostrophe replaces the letter *o*.

English-Language Learners
Guess Who • Lesson 6

Level Two

Catch a Dream

Name _____

▶ Say each picture name. Draw a line to match the picture names that rhyme. Then trace the words.

1.

bell   pen

2.

vet   vest

3.

ten   well

4.

nest   wet

For the Teacher Name the illustrations in each column, having children repeat after you. Suggest that they say the picture names aloud softly to find the rhyming words.

 3

English-Language Learners
Catch a Dream • Lesson 1

Name _____

▶ **Blend and read each word. Circle and color the picture it names.**

1. jet

2. web

3. neck

4. hen

5. pet

For the Teacher Be sure children can name the three pictures in each row. Read the directions and go through the first row with them.

◆5◆

English-Language Learners
Catch a Dream • Lesson 1

Name _____

▶ **Write the word that completes each sentence.**

was	her	said
with	every	day

1. The cat is _____ pet.

2. She plays _____ her cat.

3. She fed the cat _____ day.

For the Teacher Make up sentences about the pictures at the top of the page. *For example, The boy was a baby; The girl said yes.* Use the high-frequency words in your sentences.

6

English-Language Learners
Catch a Dream • Lesson 1

Name _____

▶ **Write the word from the box that names each picture.**

| jet | belt | wet | net | nest | bell |

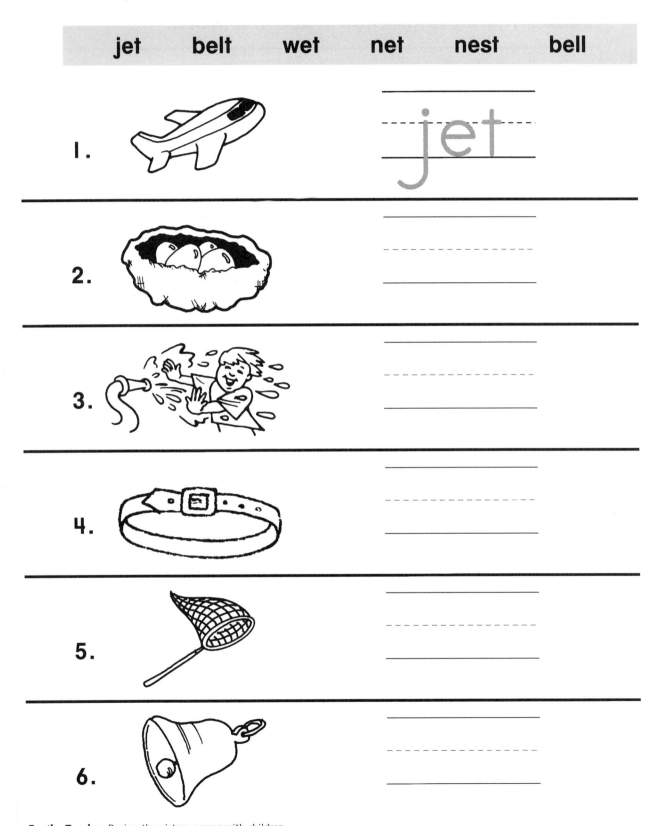

1. jet

2. _____

3. _____

4. _____

5. _____

6. _____

For the Teacher Review the picture names with children. Then have them read the words in the box. When they have completed the page, have them identify the words with short *e*.

7

English-Language Learners
Catch a Dream • Lesson 1

Name _____

▶ **Look at each picture story. What is the setting? Circle and color the picture that shows the setting. Then trace the word.**

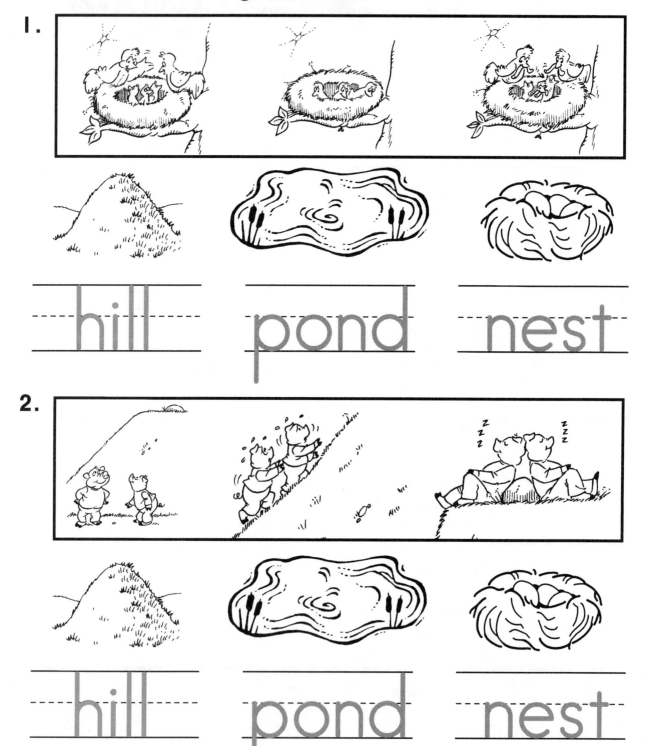

1.

hill   pond   nest

2.

hill   pond   nest

For the Teacher Give a brief description of what is happening in the first set of pictures. Tell children to pay attention to *where* the story is taking place. Write the word *where* on the board and have children circle the picture that shows where the story takes place. Repeat for the second set.

8

English-Language Learners
Catch a Dream • Lesson 1

Name _____

▶ **Say the names of the pictures in each row. Circle and color the two pictures whose names start with the same sounds.**

1.

2.

3.

4.

For the Teacher Be sure children can identify all the pictures in each row before asking them to complete the page.

◆**9**◆

English-Language Learners
Catch a Dream • Lesson 1

▶ **Write the word from the box that names each picture.**

| them | thin | bath | with | path |

1. bath

2. _____

3. _____

4. _____

5. _____

For the Teacher Before children complete this page, discuss the pictures with them. Make sure that they can name the word that goes with each picture.

English-Language Learners
Catch a Dream • Lesson 2

Name _____

▶ **Blend and read each word. Circle and color the picture it names.**

1. thin

2. moth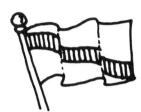

3. cloth

4. them

5. thick

For the Teacher Name the pictures in each row with children. Then have children complete the page.

◀**13**▶

English-Language Learners
Catch a Dream • Lesson 2

Name _____

▶ **Write the word that completes each sentence.**

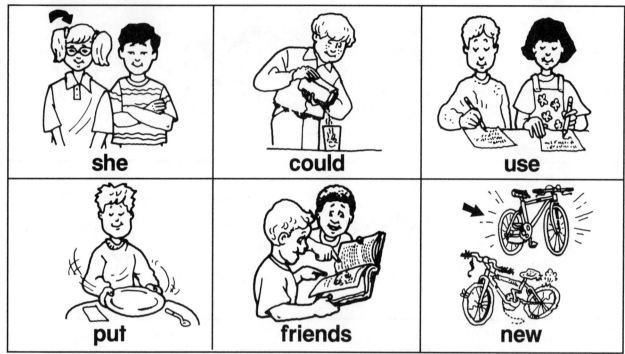

she   could   use

put   friends   new

could   put

_____

- - - - - - - - - - - - - -

1. She _____ skip rocks.

friends   use

_____

- - - - - - - - - - - - - -

2. She has to _____ flat rocks.

put   new

_____

- - - - - - - - - - - - - -

3. Her friends like her _____ trick.

For the Teacher Use the pictures at the top of the page to make up sentences for the high-frequency words. For example: *She has glasses; We use pencils for writing.*

 14

English-Language Learners
Catch a Dream • Lesson 2

▶ **Say the name of each picture. Write the picture names.**

bath	thin	path	math	thick

1. ____ ____ ____ ____
      ---- ---- ---- ----
      ____ ____ ____ ____

2. ____ ____ ____ ____
      ---- ---- ---- ----
      ____ ____ ____ ____

3.
$$\begin{array}{r} 2 \\ +1 \\ \hline 3 \end{array}$$

      ____ ____ ____ ____
      ---- ---- ---- ----
      ____ ____ ____ ____

4. ____ ____ ____ ____
      ---- ---- ---- ----
      ____ ____ ____ ____

5. ____ ____ ____ ____
      ---- ---- ---- ----
      ____ ____ ____ ____

For the Teacher Preview the page with children, naming the illustrations as necessary. Ask children where they hear the sound /th/ —at the beginning or at the end.

15

English-Language Learners
Catch a Dream • Lesson 2

▶ **Write the word that completes each sentence.**

dent	**nest**	**rest**	**vest**	**tent**

_____
- - - - - - - - - - -

1. She wants her _____.

_____
- - - - - - - - - - -

2. Here is a _____.

_____
- - - - - - - - - - -

3. Let's set up the _____.

_____
- - - - - - - - - - -

4. Oh, no! The can has a _____.

_____
- - - - - - - - - - -

5. Now we can _____!

For the Teacher Read aloud the words at the top of the page. Have children repeat after you. Remind children that the words and pictures at the top of the page can help them as they complete the sentences.

English-Language Learners
Catch a Dream • Lesson 2

Name _____

▶ **Write the word from the box that names each picture.**

skunk   bug   hump   sun   tub   bus   mug   rug   cub

1.

_____
- - - - - - - - - - -
_____

2.

_____
- - - - - - - - - - -
_____

3.

_____
- - - - - - - - - - -
_____

4.

_____
- - - - - - - - - - -
_____

5.

_____
- - - - - - - - - - -
_____

6.

_____
- - - - - - - - - - -
_____

7.

_____
- - - - - - - - - - -
_____

8.

_____
- - - - - - - - - - -
_____

9.

_____
- - - - - - - - - - -
_____

For the Teacher Preview the page with children. Help them name the pictures and read the words in the box. Then have them complete the page.

English-Language Learners
Catch a Dream • Lesson 3

▶ **Draw lines to match the picture names that rhyme. Then trace the words.**

1.

cut

bump

2.

run

nut

3.

hump

bug

4.

hug

sun

For the Teacher Have children read the picture names in each column. Suggest that they say the words softly as they look for rhyming words.

20

English-Language Learners
Catch a Dream • Lesson 3

Name _____

▶ **Circle the word that completes each sentence. Then write the word.**

your

out

says

he

gives

night

people

when

_____

1. _____ pup got out of his bed.

People
Your
He

2. He likes to come out at _____.

people
night
when

3. Mom _____ we have to give him a bath.

when
out
says

For the Teacher Use the pictures at the top of the page to make up sentences for the high-frequency words. Read and point to each word and have children do the same.

◀21▶

English-Language Learners
Catch a Dream • Lesson 3

Name _____

▶ **Read the word. Circle and color the picture it names.**

1. hen

2. duck

3. bed

4. desk

5. jump

For the Teacher Name the three pictures in each row. Then have children read the word at the left and circle and color the corresponding picture.

22

English-Language Learners
Catch a Dream • Lesson 3

Name _____

▶ **Read each word. Circle and color the picture whose name starts with the same sounds.**

1. frog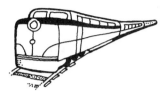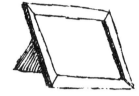

2. crib

3. grin

4. trick

5. grass

6. crab

For the Teacher Name the pictures in each row. Encourage children to say the picture names aloud as they look for matching initial sounds.

◀23▶

English-Language Learners
Catch a Dream • Lesson 3

Name _____

▶ **Say the name of each picture. Then write the word. Each new word will have three or more letters from the word before it.**

wing	sing	king	swing	ring

1.

k i n g

2.

3.

4.

5.

For the Teacher Preview the page with children. Discuss each illustration using the word it illustrates. Encourage children to practice reading the words when they have completed the page.

English-Language Learners
Catch a Dream • Lesson 4

Name _____

► **Write the word from the box that completes each sentence.**

sing	ring	king	wing	sting

_____

- - - - - - - - -

1. I am a _____ .

_____

- - - - - - - - -

2. It is a _____ .

_____

- - - - - - - - -

3. It has a _____ .

_____

- - - - - - - - -

4. We like to _____ .

_____

- - - - - - - - -

5. It is going to _____ him!

For the Teacher Discuss the illustrations and make sure children can identify what is happening in each one. Help them read the words at the top of the page.

27

English-Language Learners
Catch a Dream • Lesson 4

Name _____

▶ **Write the word that completes each sentence.**

gone

or

eat

from

two

_____

1. Bob has _____ frogs.

_____

2. A frog grows if it can _____ bugs.

_____

3. Bob got his frogs _____ a friend.

_____

4. Where have the frogs _____ ?

For the Teacher Use the pictures at the top of the page to make up sentences for the high-frequency words. Read each word and have children repeat after you. As needed, read the example sentences with children before they complete the page.

English-Language Learners
Catch a Dream • Lesson 4

Name _____

▶ **Write the word from the box that names each picture.**

| swing | skunk | bring | ring | stop | grass |

1.

_____

- - - - - - - - - - - -

_____

2.

_____

- - - - - - - - - - - -

_____

3.

_____

- - - - - - - - - - - -

_____

4.

_____

- - - - - - - - - - - -

_____

5.

_____

- - - - - - - - - - - -

_____

6.

_____

- - - - - - - - - - - -

_____

For the Teacher Review the picture names with children. Then have them read the words in the box before completing the page.

29

English-Language Learners
Catch a Dream • Lesson 4

Name _____

▶ **Look at the big picture. Make a list of things from the boxes that you can see in the big picture.**

frog

duck

eggs

chicks

pig

_____

_____

_____

_____

_____

_____

_____

_____

For the Teacher Ask volunteers to describe what they see in the picture. Ask questions to help children notice details of the scene.

◀30▶

English-Language Learners
Catch a Dream • Lesson 4

► **Write the contraction that completes each sentence.**

can't	He'll	He's	isn't	They'll

He is
_____

- - - - - - - - - - - - - - - - - - - -

I. _____ calling Bill.

---

is not
_____

- - - - - - - - - - - - - - - - - - - -

2. Bill _____ picking up.

He will
_____

- - - - - - - - - - - - - - - - - - - -

3. _____ look for Bill.

---

can not
_____

- - - - - - - - - - - - - - - - - - - -

4. He _____ see Bill.

They will
_____

- - - - - - - - - - - - - - - - - - - -

5. _____ play with the ball.

For the Teacher Talk with children about the pictures. As needed, read the example sentences with children before asking them to complete the page.

31

English-Language Learners
Catch a Dream • Lesson 4

Name _____

▶ **Blend and read each word. Circle and color the picture it names.**

1. horn

2. snore

3. stork

4. cork

5. corn

For the Teacher Name the pictures in each row. Then have children read the word at the left and circle the corresponding picture.

◄33►

English-Language Learners
Catch a Dream • Lesson 5

Name _____

▶ **Write the word from the box that names each picture.**

| cord | corn | fork | fort | snore | sport |

1.

_____

- - - - - - - - - - - -

_____

2.

_____

- - - - - - - - - - - -

_____

3.

_____

- - - - - - - - - - - -

_____

4.

_____

- - - - - - - - - - - -

_____

5.

_____

- - - - - - - - - - - -

_____

6.

_____

- - - - - - - - - - - -

_____

For the Teacher Review the picture names with children. Have them read the words in the box. Read the directions with them and have them complete the page.

◀35▶

English-Language Learners
Catch a Dream • Lesson 5

Name _____

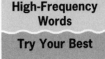
► **Write the word from the top of the page that completes each sentence.**

today

try

time

need

be

our

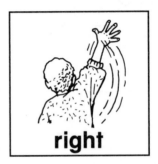

right

saw

1. This is _____ big day!

2. Mr. Gruck said, "Just _____ your best."

3. Today we _____ to be good!

For the Teacher Use the pictures at the top of the page to make up sentences for the high-frequency words. Read each word and have children repeat after you.

English-Language Learners

Catch a Dream • Lesson 5

Name _____

▶ **Write the word from the box that completes each sentence.**

fort	corn	horn	for	torn

1. This is _____ you.

2. It is not _____ .

3. It is a _____ .

4. They eat some _____ .

5. We can play in the _____ .

For the Teacher Discuss the pictures with children. Then have them read the words in the box and the sentence frames. Read the directions with them, and have them complete the page.

English-Language Learners
Catch a Dream • Lesson 5

Name _____

▶ **Look at the pictures in the big box. Then look at the pictures below the box. Circle the picture of the main character. Draw boxes around the pictures of other story characters.**

For the Teacher Invite children to tell a story based on the pictures. Ask volunteers to identify the main character and the two other characters in the story.

38

▶ **Cut out the words. Paste the words to make compound words that match the pictures.**

1. sun ☐   pack

2. ☐ mill   play

3. ☐ pen   corn

4. pop ☐   ball

5. back ☐ set

6. soft ☐  wind

For the Teacher Discuss each illustration and elicit from children what each one represents. Read the directions with children and have them complete the page.

39

English-Language Learners
Catch a Dream • Lesson 5

Name _____

▶ **Say the names of the pictures in each row. Circle the pictures whose names begin like <u>shut</u> or end like <u>wish</u>.**

1.

dish   cat   flash   box

2.

ship   hill   pan   shell

3.

nest   brush   shack   castle

4.

   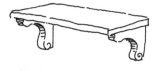

dog   shorts   cat   shelf

For the Teacher Give examples of pairs of words in which one word begins or ends with the /sh/ sound. Have children identify the word that has the /sh/ sound.

English-Language Learners
Catch a Dream • Lesson 6

Name _____

▶ **Blend and read each word. Circle the picture it names.**

1. shack

2. crash

3. splash

4. brush

5. blush

6. shell

For the Teacher Name the pictures in each row. Then demonstrate how to read the word at the left and circle the corresponding picture.

◀43▶

English-Language Learners
Catch a Dream • Lesson 6

Name _____

▶ **Write the word or words that complete the sentence.**

some

their

many

how

away

hide

funny

1. I got _____ new fish.

2. How _____ fish did you get?

3. Some _____ to get _____ from the big ones.

4. _____ tricks are _____.

For the Teacher Talk with children about the pictures at the top of the page. Read each word and have children repeat after you. As needed, read the sentences with children before asking them to complete the page.

English-Language Learners
Catch a Dream • Lesson 6

▶ **Say the name of each picture. Write the word in the boxes. Each word will either begin or end with <u>sh</u>.**

ship	dish	shop	shelf	fish

1.

2.

3.

4.

5.

For the Teacher Preview the page with children. Discuss each illustration, using the word it illustrates. Be sure children understand the task before they complete the page.

45

▶ **Look at the big picture. Then read the sentences. Circle the sentences that tell about the picture.**

The cat is big.

The cat is looking at the dog.

The dog is on the rug.

The lamp is on.

English-Language Learners
Catch a Dream • Lesson 6

Name _____

▶ **Write the word that completes each sentence.**

slid	**trunk**	**sled**	**drum**	**scarf**

1. Gwen will pack her _____ for her trip.

2. She will bring her _____.

3. She will need a _____.

4. She will go on a _____.

5. Gwen _____ down the hill.

For the Teacher Use the words as you discuss the pictures at the top of the page. Have volunteers read the incomplete sentences before children complete the page.

 47

English-Language Learners
Catch a Dream • Lesson 6

· T R O P H I E S ·

Level Three

Here and There

Name _____

▶ **Say both picture names. Circle the picture whose name has the beginning sound for <u>ch</u>.**

1.

2.

3.

4.

5.

6.

7.

8.

For the Teacher Say each picture name, and have children repeat it. Say *chin* and repeat the /ch/ sound. Tell children to listen for that sound in each picture name and circle the picture name with that sound.

3

English-Language Learners
Here and There • Lesson 1

▶ **Read each word. Circle the picture it names.**

1. chin

2. chop

3. chick

4. pitch

5. catch

6. match $$\begin{array}{r} 2 \\ +1 \\ \hline 3 \end{array}$$

For the Teacher Be sure children know the names of the pictures in each row. Read each word aloud and have children repeat the word after you.

5

English-Language Learners
Here and There • Lesson 1

Name _____

▶ **Write the word that completes each
sentence.**

fly

animals

turns

around

_____

- - - - - - - - - - - - - - - -

1. I like _____ .

_____

- - - - - - - - - - - - - - - -

2. They live all _____ me.

_____

- - - - - - - - - - - - - - - -

3. Soon some will _____
in the air.

_____

- - - - - - - - - - - - - - - -

4. The fox _____ back
to look at me.

6

English-Language Learners
Here and There • Lesson 1

Name _____

► **Circle the word that goes with each picture.**

1.

cat   catch

2.

fish   fan

3.

hush   help

4.

milk   match

5.

pants   pitch

6.

hand   hatch

For the Teacher Review each picture name with children. Then have them read the words. When they have completed the page, have them identify the words with /ch/ and the words with /sh/.

English-Language Learners
Here and There • Lesson 1

► **Say each picture name. Listen to the beginning sounds. Circle the two letters that stand for the beginning sounds.**

1.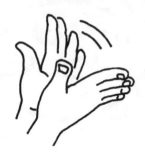

clap

2.

flag

3.

plant

4.

plum

5.

clock

6.

plus

7.

flash

8.

sled

9.

clip

English-Language Learners
Here and There • Lesson 1

Name _____

▶ **Say both picture names. Circle the picture whose name has the vowel sound you hear in the word <u>car</u>.**

1.

2.

3.

4.

5.

6.

7.

8.

For the Teacher Name each picture and have children repeat the name. Say *car* and repeat the /är/ sound. Tell children to listen for that sound in the picture names. Then have them circle one picture in each pair.

English-Language Learners
Here and There • Lesson 2

Name _____

► **Read each word. Circle and color the picture it names.**

1. star

2. car

3. jar

4. arm

5. dart
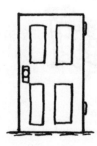  

For the Teacher Name the three pictures in each row.
Then have children complete the page.

12

English-Language Learners
Here and There • Lesson 2

Name _____

▶ **Write the word from the box that best completes each sentence.**

house

take

there

city

1. Will you _____ the bag to Mr. Hill?

_____
- - - - - - - - - - - - -

2. He lives in a little _____ on his farm.

_____
- - - - - - - - - - - - -

3. Sometimes he takes a trip

to the _____.

_____
- - - - - - - - - - - - -

4. "I like it _____," says Mr. Hill.

_____
- - - - - - - - - - - - -

For the Teacher Talk with children about the words and pictures at the top of the page. Talk about the pictures using the words. Let volunteers read the incomplete sentences aloud, and then have children complete the sentences.

13

English-Language Learners
Here and There • Lesson 2

Name _____

▶ **Circle the word that completes each sentence. Then write the word.**

1.  Bart is in a _____.

car
can

2.  Bart is on the _____.

bed
bars

3.  Bart can use a _____.

chin
cart

4.  Bart has a big _____.

fork
flag

5. Bart can play a _____.

horn
horse

For the Teacher Help children name the objects in each picture and read the sentences and words. Then have children complete the page.

14

English-Language Learners
Here and There • Lesson 2

Name _____

▶ **Look at each big picture. Think of a story that goes with the picture. Circle the little picture that shows the best place for the story.**

1.

2.

For the Teacher Remind children that the setting is the place where a story happens. Discuss with children what is taking place in each boxed picture. Then use place names for each set of smaller images.

15

English-Language Learners
Here and There • Lesson 2

Name _____

► **Finish each sentence. Put together the word and the word ending above the line. Write the new word on the line.**

jump + s

_____

- - - - - - - - - - - - - - - - - - - -

1. Jen _____ up and down.

jump + ing

_____

- - - - - - - - - - - - - - - - - - - -

2. Her friend is _____, too.

walk + ing

_____

- - - - - - - - - - - - - - - - - - - -

3. He is not _____ now.

walk + ed

_____

- - - - - - - - - - - - - - - - - - - -

4. Then Jen _____ a little more.

For the Teacher Have volunteers tell what the children in the pictures are doing. With children, complete each sentence orally. Then have children say and write the words.

16

English-Language Learners
Here and There • Lesson 2

Name _____

▶ **Say each picture name. Listen to the beginning sounds. Circle the picture whose name starts with the letters shown.**

1. qu

2. qu

3. qu

4. wh

5. wh

6. wh

For the Teacher With children, review the sounds—/kw/, /hw/—qu and wh. Name the three pictures in the row. Then have children complete the page.

18

English-Language Learners
Here and There • Lesson 3

Name _____

▶ **Circle and color the picture that goes with each word.**

1. quilt

2. which

3. when

4. quiz

 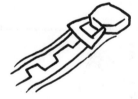 

5. quack

For the Teacher Name the three pictures in each row.
Then have children read the words at the left and
complete the page.

20

English-Language Learners
Here and There • Lesson 3

Name _____

▶ **Write the word from the top of the page that completes each sentence.**

 **read**　 **books**　 **family**　 **writing**

_____

1. Her _____ helps her work.

_____

2. They _____ books
about animals.

_____

3. The best _____ are by
Beth Chan.

_____

4. She is _____ about a dog.

For the Teacher Use the high-frequency words as you talk with children about the pictures at the top of the page. Read each word and have children repeat it. Then have children complete the sentences.

21

English-Language Learners
Here and There • Lesson 3

Name _____

▶ **Circle the word that completes each sentence. Then write the word.**

quick   quiz
_____

- - - - - - - - - - - - -

1. Whit is _____.

fill   quit
_____

- - - - - - - - - - - - -

2. She will not _____.

whip   what
_____

- - - - - - - - - - - - -

3. Look _____ she can do.

Which   West
_____

- - - - - - - - - - - - -

4. _____ one will she do next?

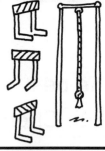

this   tent
_____

- - - - - - - - - - - - -

5. Is _____ for Whit?

For the Teacher Help children describe what is happening in each picture, and have a volunteer read aloud the first sentence. Have children complete the page.

22

English-Language Learners
Here and There • Lesson 3

Name _____

▶ **Look at the pictures in the box. Then look at the pictures that show characters. Circle the picture of the main character. Make check marks above the pictures of other characters.**

For the Teacher Have children make up a story about the pictures in the box. Be sure children understand what they are to do before having them complete the page.

23

English-Language Learners
Here and There • Lesson 3

Name _____

► **Circle the picture that goes with each word.**

1. flag

2. clock

3. plant

4. sled

5. clip

6. plus

For the Teacher Name the three pictures in each row. Then have children read the words at the left and complete the page.

24

English-Language Learners
Here and There • Lesson 3

Name _____

▶ **Say the picture name. Circle and color each picture whose name has the vowel sound /ûr/.**

purr

1.

2.

3.

4.

5.

6.

7.

8.

For the Teacher Say *purr* and have children repeat the word. Help children name each picture. Then have children listen for the /ûr/ sound as they say each picture name.

26

English-Language Learners
Here and There • Lesson 4

Name _____

▶ **Read each word. Circle and color the picture it names.**

1. stir

2. bird

3. curl

4. fern

5. girl

For the Teacher Be sure children can name the pictures in each row. Read the words aloud with children repeating after you. Then have children complete the page.

28

English-Language Learners
Here and There • Lesson 4

Name _____

▶ **Write the word that completes each sentence.**

	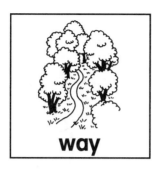		
four	**way**	**find**	**full**

1. Peg found the _____ to the pond.

2. These _____ friends were glad to follow her.

3. The pond was _____ of little fish.

4. Will her friends _____ the pond next time?

For the Teacher Use the high-frequency words as you talk with children about the pictures at the top of the page. Have children repeat each word after you. Let volunteers read the incomplete sentences aloud, and then have children complete the sentences.

English-Language Learners
Here and There • Lesson 4

Name _____

▶ **Circle the word that names each picture.**

1.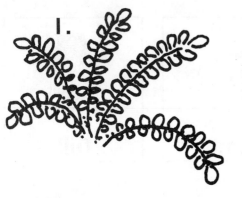

fern
fish

2.

turn
tusk

3.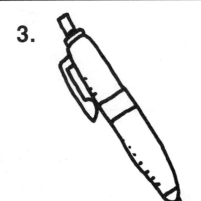

park
pen

4.

curl
kick

5.

bell
bird

6.

burn
bus

7.

vest
bird

8.

tank
turn

For the Teacher With children, name the pictures. Have a volunteer read aloud the words in the first exercise. Then have children complete the page.

30

Name _____

▶ **Look at each big picture. Circle the little picture that shows where the story takes place.**

1.

2.

For the Teacher Remind children that the setting is the place where a story happens. Discuss the boxed pictures with children. Then use place words to talk about the answer choices before children complete the page.

31

English-Language Learners
Here and There • Lesson 4

Name _____

▶ **Put together the word and the word ending above the lines. Write the new word to complete the sentence.**

look + s

_____

- - - - - - - - - - - - - - - - - - - -

1. Nick _____ in the barn.

look + ed

_____

- - - - - - - - - - - - - - - - - - - -

2. Then he _____ in the yard.

look + ing

_____

- - - - - - - - - - - - - - - - - - - -

3. Now he is _____ in the little house.

find + s

_____

- - - - - - - - - - - - - - - - - - - -

4. He _____ his dog there!

For the Teacher Help children read the sentences. Guide them through the first item, and have them complete the page.

32

English-Language Learners
Here and There • Lesson 4

Name _____

▶ **Say both picture names. Circle the picture whose name ends with the sound for <u>le</u>.**

1.

2.

3.

4.

5.

6.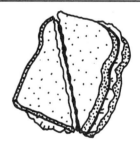

7.

8.

For the Teacher Name each picture and have children
repeat the name. Say *giggle* and repeat the /əl/ sound.
Ask children to listen for that sound as they name each
pair of pictures.

34

English-Language Learners
Here and There • Lesson 5

Name _____

▶ **Read each word. Circle and color the picture it names.**

1. bubble

2. pickle

3. candle

4. turtle

5. juggle

6. rattle

For the Teacher Name the three pictures in each row. Then have children read the word at the left and circle the corresponding picture.

36

English-Language Learners
Here and There • Lesson 5

Name _____

▶ **Write the word that completes each
sentence.**

talk

together

school

place

1. We can walk _____ .

_____

2. We will _____
to each other on the way.

3. This park is a great _____ .

4. Here we are at _____ .

For the Teacher Talk with children about the pictures at
the top of the page. Use each word in a sentence about
the picture. Read each word and have children repeat it.

37

English-Language Learners
Here and There • Lesson 5

▶ **Write the word that completes each sentence.**

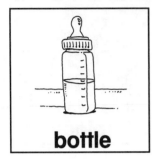
bottle

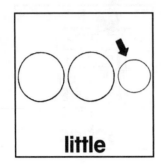
little

rattle

tickle

1. They are big, and
_____
- - - - - - - - - - - - - -
I am _____.

_____
- - - - - - - - - - - - - -
2. I play with my _____.

_____
- - - - - - - - - - - - - -
3. I drink from a _____.

_____
- - - - - - - - - - - - - -
4. She likes to _____ me.

For the Teacher With children, read aloud the boxed words and describe the pictures. Have volunteers read the incomplete sentences aloud. Then have children complete the sentences.

English-Language Learners
Here and There • Lesson 5

▶ **Put together the word and the word
ending above the lines. Write the new
word to complete the sentence.**

small + er

_____

- -

I. My dog is _____
than my cat.

small + est

_____

- -

2. My rat is the _____ of all.

fast + er

_____

- -

3. My rat runs _____
than my cat.

fast + est

_____

- -

4. My dog runs the _____ of all.

For the Teacher Help children describe the animals in
each picture, and have volunteers read the incomplete
sentences aloud. Then have children combine the word
and word ending to complete each sentence.

English-Language Learners
Here and There • Lesson 5

Name _____

▶ **Say the picture names in each row. Circle and color the pictures whose names rhyme.**

1.

2.

3.

4.

For the Teacher Say examples of rhyming words with the long *o* sound, such as *grow* and *low*. Have children repeat the rhyming words. With children, name the pictures in each row.

41

English-Language Learners
Here and There • Lesson 6

Name _____

► **Read each word. Circle and color the picture it names.**

1. boat

2. snow

3. bowl

4. coat

5. road

6. goat

For the Teacher Name the three pictures in each row. Then have children read the word at the left and circle the corresponding picture.

43

English-Language Learners
Here and There • Lesson 6

Name _____

▶ **Write the word from the box that
completes each sentence.**

made

door

kind

Would

_____

- - - - - - - - - - - -

1. Who is at the _____?

_____

- - - - - - - - - - - -

2. _____ you like to come in?

_____

- - - - - - - - - - - -

3. I _____ this for you.

_____

- - - - - - - - - - - -

4. How _____ of you!

For the Teacher Use the high-frequency words as you
talk with children about the pictures at the top of the
page. Have children repeat the words after you.

44

English-Language Learners
Here and There • Lesson 6

Name _____

▶ **Circle the word that names each picture.**

1.

road
row

2.

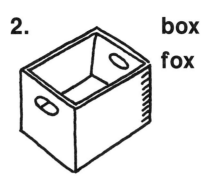

box
fox

3.

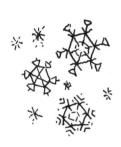

soap
snow

4.

gum
goat

5.

box
bowl

6.

fan
fox

7.

pot
pig

8.

boat
Bob

For the Teacher Help children name the pictures, and have volunteers read aloud the pairs of words. After children have completed the page, have them tell which words have the long *o* sound and which have the short *o* sound.

45

English-Language Learners
Here and There • Lesson 6

Name _____

► **Circle the word that shows how each character feels.**

1.

mad   glad

2.

mad   glad

3.

glad   sad

4.

glad   sad

5.

mad   glad

6.

sad   glad

For the Teacher With children, talk about feelings story characters sometimes have. Ask what might make a story character feel glad, sad, or mad. Then read the directions to children and have them complete the page.

English-Language Learners
Here and There • Lesson 6

Name _____

▶ **Put together the word and the word ending above the line. Write the new word to complete the sentence.**

call + ed

_____

- - - - - - - - - - - - - - - - -

1. Lin _____ Hal.

---

talk + ed

_____

- - - - - - - - - - - - - - - - -

2. They _____ for a long time.

---

call + ing

_____

- - - - - - - - - - - - - - - - -

3. Now Lin is _____ Deb.

---

like + s

_____

- - - - - - - - - - - - - - - - -

4. Lin _____ to call her friends.

For the Teacher *Have children describe what is happening in each picture. Read the incomplete sentences with children, having them fill in the missing verb form. Then have children complete the sentences.*

English-Language Learners
Here and There • Lesson 6

► **Write the word that names each picture.**

| bee | beach | eat | free | he | leap | peach | sleep | she |

1.

_____
- - - - - - - - -
_____

2.

_____
- - - - - - - - -
_____

3.

_____
- - - - - - - - -
_____

4.

_____
- - - - - - - - -
_____

5.

_____
- - - - - - - - -
_____

6.

_____
- - - - - - - - -
_____

7.

_____
- - - - - - - - -
_____

8.

_____
- - - - - - - - -
_____

9.

_____
- - - - - - - - -
_____

For the Teacher Review the picture names with children. Then have them read the words in the box. Finally, have them complete the page.

9

English-Language Learners
Time Together • Lesson 1

Name _____

▶ **Look at the picture. Then complete the sentence by writing a word from the box that has the long sound of e.**

| beets | beak | sleeve | beads | seal |

1.

_____

_ _ _ _ _ _ _ _ _ _ _ _ _ _ _ _ _ _ _

Ann strings _____.

2.

_____

_ _ _ _ _ _ _ _ _ _ _ _ _ _ _ _ _ _ _

Don has some _____.

3.

_____

_ _ _ _ _ _ _ _ _ _ _ _ _ _ _ _ _ _ _

This bird has a big _____.

4.

_____

_ _ _ _ _ _ _ _ _ _ _ _ _ _ _ _ _ _ _

The _____ has a ball.

5.

_____

_ _ _ _ _ _ _ _ _ _ _ _ _ _ _ _ _ _ _

The _____ is torn.

For the Teacher Preview the page with children.
Discuss each illustration, using the word it illustrates.
Then read aloud the directions and have children
complete the page.

11

English-Language Learners
Time Together • Lesson 1

Name _____

▶ **Write the word that completes each sentence.**

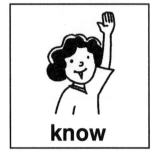**know**	**those**	**write**	**room**

_____
- - - - - - - - - - - - - - - - - -

1. Bob and Jim _____.
   Doris knows, also.

2. They moved only one of

   _____
   - - - - - - - - - - - -
   _____ desks.

_____
- - - - - - - - - - - - - - - -

3. He should _____ a
   thank-you note.

4. You can find anything in

   _____
   - - - - - - - - - - - -

   Bob's _____.

For the Teacher Talk with children about the pictures at the top of the page. Read each word and have children repeat it. Let volunteers read the incomplete sentences aloud, and then have children complete the sentences.

12

Name _____

▶ **Write the word from the box that matches the picture.**

coat	beach	bowl	teach	coach	read

1.

_____

- - - - - - - - - - - - - - - - - -

_____

2.

_____

- - - - - - - - - - - - - - - - - -

_____

3.

_____

- - - - - - - - - - - - - - - - - -

_____

4.

_____

- - - - - - - - - - - - - - - - - -

_____

5.

_____

- - - - - - - - - - - - - - - - - -

_____

6.

_____

- - - - - - - - - - - - - - - - - -

_____

For the Teacher Preview the page with children. Discuss each illustration, using the word it illustrates. Then have children complete the page.

13

English-Language Learners
Time Together • Lesson 1

Name _____

▶ **Write the words in each row in ABC order.**

1.

cat

_____
- - - - - - - - - - - -
_____

bird

_____
- - - - - - - - - - - -
_____

dog

_____
- - - - - - - - - - - -
_____

2.

hen

_____
- - - - - - - - - - - -
_____

duck

_____
- - - - - - - - - - - -
_____

frog

_____
- - - - - - - - - - - -
_____

3.

toad

_____
- - - - - - - - - - - -
_____

goat

_____
- - - - - - - - - - - -
_____

fish

_____
- - - - - - - - - - - -
_____

For the Teacher Review the alphabet with children.
Write it on the board, or point it out on a classroom wall.
Help children read the words in each row, and have them
point to the first letter in each word.

14

English-Language Learners
Time Together • Lesson 1

Name _____

► **Read each pair of sentences. Complete the second sentence by writing the contraction for the underlined words in the first sentence.**

1. <u>She is</u> looking at cats.

_____

- - - - - - - - - - - - - - - - - - -

_____ going to get a new cat.

2. She <u>does not</u> want a dog.

_____

- - - - - - - - - - - - - - - - - - -

She _____ have room for a dog.

3. <u>She will</u> take this little cat.

_____

- - - - - - - - - - - - - - - - - - -

_____ brush it every day.

4. <u>He is</u> glad the cat will have a home.

_____

- - - - - - - - - - - - - - - - - - -

_____ going to miss that cat.

For the Teacher Talk with children about the pictures. Read the sentences and discuss with the children how the underlined words can be combined to form contractions. Have them complete the page.

15

English-Language Learners
Time Together • Lesson 1

► **Write the word from the box that completes each sentence.**

| race | grapes | Jane | lake | caves |

1.

Dora went to the _____.

2.

She ate some _____.

3.

She looked at a book about _____.

4.

Soon _____ came to see Dora.

5.

They had a _____ around the lake.

For the Teacher Read the words in the box, making sure that the children know what each one means. When they have completed the page, have them identify all the words on the page that have the long *a* sound.

17

English-Language Learners
Time Together • Lesson 2

Name _____

▶ **Write the word from the box that names the picture.**

| cane cake cape snake game gate mane plate vase |

1.

_____
- - - - - - - - -
_____

2.

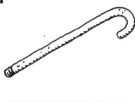

_____
- - - - - - - - -
_____

3.

_____
- - - - - - - - -
_____

4.

_____
- - - - - - - - -
_____

5.

_____
- - - - - - - - -
_____

6.

_____
- - - - - - - - -
_____

7.

_____
- - - - - - - - -
_____

8.

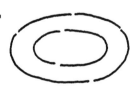

_____
- - - - - - - - -
_____

9.

_____
- - - - - - - - -
_____

For the Teacher Review the picture names with children. Then have them read the words in the box. Finally, have them complete the page.

19

English-Language Learners
Time Together • Lesson 2

Name _____

▶ **Write the word that completes the sentence.**

town

Earth

country

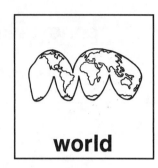
world

_____

- - - - - - - - - - - - - - -

1. This small _____ is special to Kate.

_____

- - - - - - - - - - - - - - -

2. Canada is a big _____.

_____

- - - - - - - - - - - - - - -

3. The planet _____ has many seas.

4. Planes fly all over the

_____

- - - - - - - - - - - - - - -

_____.

For the Teacher Talk with children about the pictures at the top of the page. Read each word and have children repeat it. Have volunteers read the incomplete sentences aloud, and then have children complete the sentences.

English-Language Learners
Time Together • Lesson 2

▶ **Find the picture whose name has the long sound of a. Write the picture name. Cross out the other picture.**

base	cane	pane	race	vase

1. _____
   _ _ _ _ _ _ _ _ _
   _____

2. _____
   _ _ _ _ _ _ _ _ _
   _____

3. _____
   _ _ _ _ _ _ _ _ _
   _____

4. _____
   _ _ _ _ _ _ _ _ _
   _____

5. _____
   _ _ _ _ _ _ _ _ _
   _____

For the Teacher Preview the picture names with children. Then have them read the words in the box. Read the directions and go through the first exercise with children. Finally, have them complete the page.

21

English-Language Learners
Time Together • Lesson 2

Name _____

▶ **Cut out the cards. Paste them in two groups.**

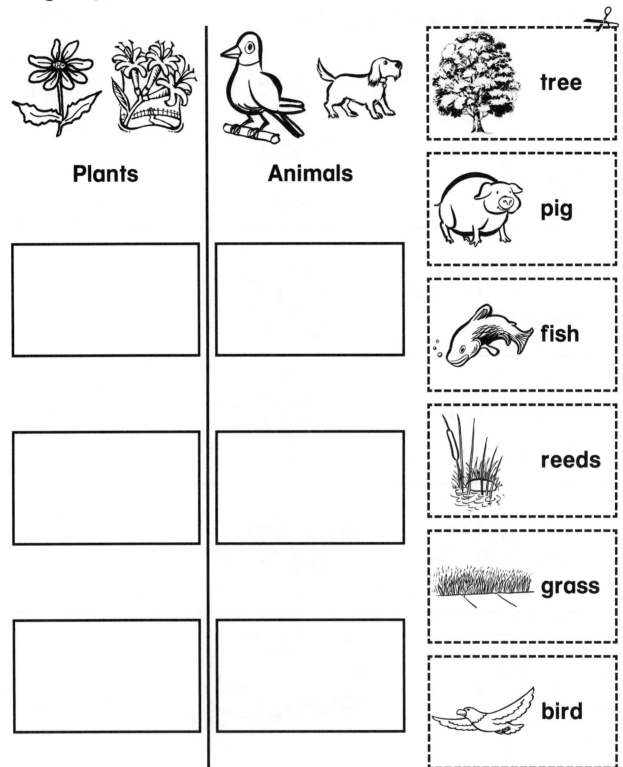

Plants | **Animals**

tree

pig

fish

reeds

grass

bird

For the Teacher Talk with children about plants and animals. Have them name different plants and animals they know. Then help children read the word on each card. Have children cut the cards out, organize them into two groups, and then paste them down.

22

▶ **Add ed and ing to each word. Remember to drop the e.**

	Add ed	**Add ing**
name	_____	_____
race	_____	_____
tame	_____	_____

▶ **Write the word that completes each sentence.**

1. Tom is _____ with Bob.

2. She _____ the big cat.

For the Teacher Talk with children about the pictures, using the words they will need to complete the page.

23

English-Language Learners
Time Together • Lesson 2

Name _____

► **Write the word from the box that names each picture.**

| happy | penny | sandy | sixty | soapy |

1. _____

2. _____

3. _____

4. _____

5. _____

For the Teacher Review the pictures with children, using the words in the box as you describe them. Then have them read the words in the box and complete the page.

English-Language Learners
Time Together • Lesson 3

► **Write the word from the box that completes each sentence.**

buggy	puppy	dirty	happy	hilly

1. Sally has a _____.

2. Betty has a baby _____.

3. Sally's pet is _____.

4. The wheel gets _____.

5. The street is _____.

For the Teacher Review the picture names with children. Then have them read the words in the box. Finally, have them complete the page.

27

English-Language Learners
Time Together • Lesson 3

Name _____

▶ **Write the word from the box that completes the sentence.**

different

water

years

hold

_____
- - - - - - - - - - - - - - - - - - -

1. People live in _____ homes.

_____
- - - - - - - - - - - - - - - - - - -

2. The _____ is warm.

_____
- - - - - - - - - - - -

3. The garden is many _____ old.

_____
- - - - - - - - - - - - - - - - - - -

4. You should _____ the umbrella above you.

For the Teacher Use the Vocabulary Words as you talk with children about the pictures at the top of the page. Have children repeat the words after you. Have children complete the sentences.

English-Language Learners
Time Together • Lesson 3

Name _____

► **Write the word from the box that completes each sentence.**

yummy	hurry	happy	party	thirty	very

1. Carly is having a _____.

2. The cake looks _____.

3. The children _____ to win the race.

4. Carly got _____ gifts.

5. The children were _____.

For the Teacher Review the pictures with children, discussing them by using the words from the box. Then have them read the words in the box before completing the page.

English-Language Learners
Time Together • Lesson 3

Name _____

▶ **Cut out the cards. Paste them in two groups.**

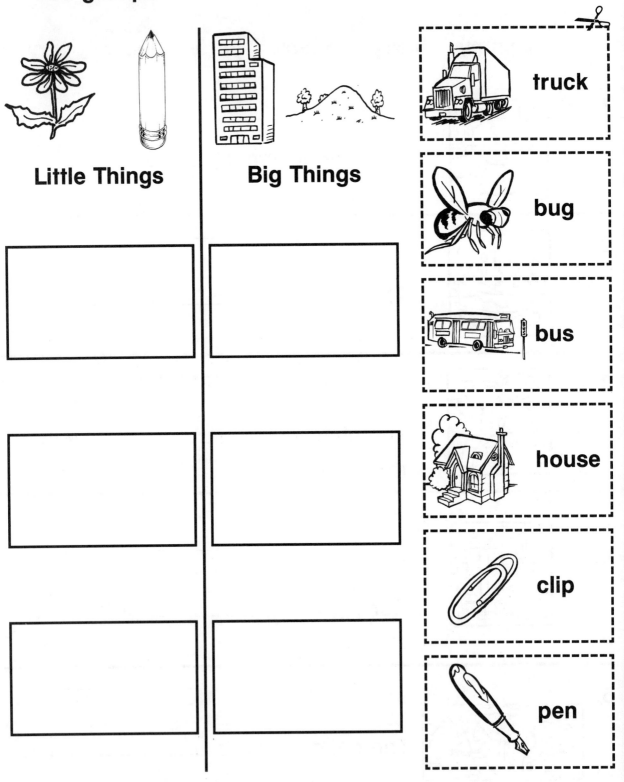

Little Things   **Big Things**

truck

bug

bus

house

clip

pen

For the Teacher Ask children to name familiar things that are little and big. Help children read the word on each card. Then have children cut out the cards, organize them into two groups, and paste them down.

English-Language Learners
Time Together • Lesson 3

▶ **Write the word from the box that completes each sentence.**

| cities | cried | flies | tried | studied |

_____
- - - - - - - - - - - - - -
1. They _____ their best.

_____
- - - - - - - - - - - - - -
2. The bird _____ in the air.

_____
- - - - - - - - - - - - - -
3. He _____ hard for the test.

_____
- - - - - - - - - - - - - -
4. They like to go to big _____ .

_____
- - - - - - - - - - - - - -
5. The baby _____ for his bottle.

For the Teacher Talk with children about the words in the box. As needed, read the example sentences with children before asking them to complete the page.

31

English-Language Learners
Time Together • Lesson 3

▶ **Write the word from the box that goes with the picture.**

bike	dive	hive	lime	nine	pine	ride	time	vine

1.

2.

3.

4.

5.

6.

7.

8.

9.

For the Teacher Talk with children about each picture, using the corresponding word from the box as you do so. Read each word and have children repeat it. Then have children complete the page.

33

English-Language Learners
Time Together • Lesson 4

► **Write the word from the box that answers the question or completes the sentence.**

| bride | hive | like | ride | white |

_____
\- - - - - - - - - -

1. Where do bees live? _____

_____
\- - - - - - - - - -

2. You _____ your friends. _____

_____
\- - - - - - - - - -

3. A _____ on a bus can be fun. _____

_____
\- - - - - - - - - -

4. Who has a wedding? _____

_____
\- - - - - - - - - -

5. What is the color of snow? _____

For the Teacher Talk with children about each picture, using the corresponding word from the box as you do so. Then read each word in the box and have children repeat it before asking them to complete the page.

35

English-Language Learners
Time Together • Lesson 4

Name _____

▶ **Write the word that completes the sentence.**

 **picture**  **young**  **listen**  **cook**

_____
- - - - - - - - - - - - - - - - -

1. They _____ because they are hungry.

_____
- - - - - - - - - - - - - - - - -

2. They _____ for someone at the front door.

_____
- - - - - - - - - - - - - - - - -

3. We like to _____ good deserts.

_____
- - - - - - - - - - - - - - - - -

4. Most _____ people like sweets.

For the Teacher Talk with children about the pictures at the top of the page. Read each word and have children repeat it.

36

English-Language Learners
Time Together • Lesson 4

Name _____

▶ **Write the word from the box that names the picture.**

bite	dime	file	fin	hike	hit	kit	pig	rice

1.

_____

- - - - - - -

_____

2.

_____

- - - - - - -

_____

3.

_____

- - - - - - -

_____

4.

_____

- - - - - - -

_____

5.

_____

- - - - - - -

_____

6.

_____

- - - - - - -

_____

7.

_____

- - - - - - -

_____

8.

_____

- - - - - - -

_____

9.

_____

- - - - - - -

_____

For the Teacher Review the picture names with children. Then have them read the words in the box. When they have completed the page, have them identify the words with long *i* and the words with short *i*.

37

English-Language Learners
Time Together • Lesson 4

Name _____

▶ **Write the words in each row in ABC order.**

1.

mug

_____
- - - - - - - - -
_____

rug

_____
- - - - - - - - -
_____

bug

_____
- - - - - - - - -
_____

2.

sock

_____
- - - - - - - - -
_____

rock

_____
- - - - - - - - -
_____

clock

_____
- - - - - - - - -
_____

3.

van

_____
- - - - - - - - -
_____

fan

_____
- - - - - - - - -
_____

pan

_____
- - - - - - - - -
_____

For the Teacher Begin by reviewing the alphabet with children. Write it on the board, or point it out on a classroom wall. Help children read the words in each row, and have them point to the first letter in each word. Then have children write the words in alphabetical order.

38

English-Language Learners
Time Together • Lesson 4

▶ **Write the contraction for the underlined words to complete each sentence.**

1.

She is
_____
- -
_____ reading.

2.

did not
_____
- -
She _____ finish the story.

3.

They will
_____
- -
_____ eat dinner.

4.

She will
_____
- -
_____ finish the story.

For the Teacher Preview the page with children. Discuss each illustration, using the contraction that the children will use to finish the sentence. Then have children complete the page.

39

English-Language Learners
Time Together • Lesson 4

Name _____

▶ **Write the word from the box that names each picture.**

| cent | circle | city | ice | pencil | prince |

1.

_____

- - - - - - - - - - - - - - -

_____

2.

_____

- - - - - - - - - - - - - - -

_____

3.

_____

- - - - - - - - - - - - - - -

_____

4.

_____

- - - - - - - - - - - - - - -

_____

5.

_____

- - - - - - - - - - - - - - -

_____

6.

_____

- - - - - - - - - - - - - - -

_____

For the Teacher Review the picture names with children. Then have them read the words in the box and complete the page.

English-Language Learners
Time Together • Lesson 5

Name _____

▶ **Cut out the words. Paste the words to name each picture.**

1.

2.

3.

4.

5.

6.

7.

8.

9.

braces

cereal

circle

circus

dance

dice

face

rice

space

For the Teacher Discuss the pictures, using the appropriate word for each one. Read the directions to children and have them complete the page.

English-Language Learners
Time Together • Lesson 5

Name _____

▶ **Write the word from the box that completes the sentence.**

pretty

say

almost

sound

1. Spencer _____ always wins races, but not today.

2. The winner does get a _____ ribbon.

3. They _____ she will even get a T-shirt.

4. Once the race ended, the _____ of cheering filled the air.

For the Teacher Talk with children about the pictures at the top of the page. Read each word and have children repeat it. Let volunteers read the incomplete sentences aloud, and then have children complete the sentences.

44

English-Language Learners
Time Together • Lesson 5

▶ **Write the word from the box that names each picture.**

lace	mice	price	spice	space	trace

1.

_____

- - - - - - - - - - - - -

_____

2.

_____

- - - - - - - - - - - - -

_____

3.

_____

- - - - - - - - - - - - -

_____

4.

50¢

_____

- - - - - - - - - - - - -

_____

5.

_____

- - - - - - - - - - - - -

_____

6.

_____

- - - - - - - - - - - - -

_____

For the Teacher Discuss the pictures with children. Provide other examples of the words as needed. Then have them read the words in the box. When they have completed the page, have them identify the words with *ace* and the words with *ice*.

45

English-Language Learners
Time Together • Lesson 5

▶ **Circle the word that completes the sentence. Then write the word.**

1.  She likes to _____ .

   rice
   ride

2.  The _____ is low.

   price
   pride

3.  The _____ wore white.

   mice
   bride

4.  Do you like _____?

   rice
   tide

5.  It is low _____ .

   twice
   tide

For the Teacher Preview the page with children.
Discuss each illustration, using the word it illustrates.
Then have children complete the page. When they have
finished, have them identify the words with -ice and the
words with -ide.

46

English-Language Learners
Time Together • Lesson 5

Name _____

▶ **Say the names of the pictures in each row.**
Circle the pictures whose names rhyme.

I.   clown   bike   crown   tree

2.   cow   bow   dog   cat

3.   loud   lake   river   cloud

4.   sour   hour   shirt   bird

5.   shower   ball   cup   tower

For the Teacher Make sure children understand the concept of rhyming words. Ask volunteers to identify all the pictures in the row before asking children to complete the page.

48

English-Language Learners
Time Together • Lesson 6

▶ **Circle and write the word that completes the sentence. Cross out the other word.**

pound

1. **loud**   We need a _____ of flour.

crowd

2. **town**   Jim went into_____.

ground

3. **out**   He got some _____ meat.

round

4. **found**   He _____ a dollar.

flowers

5. **powders**   He got some _____.

For the Teacher Have children read the words in each sentence, making sure they understand them before they complete the page.

50

English-Language Learners
Time Together • Lesson 6

Name _____

▶ **Write the word that completes each sentence.**

busy

Dr.

care

eight

1. Jimmy has _____ pets.

2. _____ Brown is Jimmy's vet.

3. The vet is very _____.

4. She takes _____ of all Jimmy's pets.

For the Teacher Use the Vocabulary Words as you talk
with children about the pictures at the top of the page.
Have children read the words after you before they
complete the page.

51

English-Language Learners
Time Together • Lesson 6

Name _____

▶ **Write the word from the box that names each picture.**

owl	pouch	power	scouts	towel	trout

1. _____

2. _____

3. _____

4. _____

5. _____

6. _____

For the Teacher Review the picture names with children. Have them identify the words with *ou* and the words with *ow*.

English-Language Learners
Time Together • Lesson 6

► Cut out the cards. Paste them in two groups.

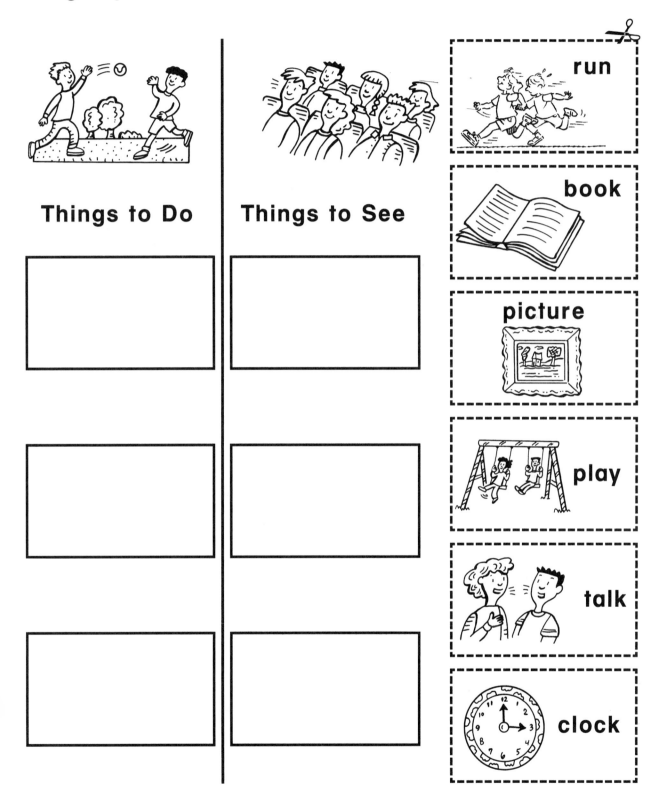

Things to Do

Things to See

run

book

picture

play

talk

clock

For the Teacher Ask children to name things they can do and things they can see. Then help children read the word on each card. Have children cut out the cards, organize them into two groups, and paste them down.

53

English-Language Learners
Time Together • Lesson 6

▶ **Write the word from the box that completes each sentence.**

clown	frown	gown	ground	round

1. _____

Sam has a _____.

2. _____

Sara is in her _____.

3. _____

Balls are _____.

4. _____

Plants grow in the _____.

5. _____

The _____ was funny.

For the Teacher Review the words in the box with children, demonstrating their meanings as needed. When they have completed the page, have children identify the words with *own* and the words with *ound*.

54

English-Language Learners
Time Together • Lesson 6

Name _____

► **Write the word from the box that names each picture.**

| cry | fries | fly | lie | pie | shy | sky | tie | why |

1.

_____

- - - - - - - - - - - -

_____

2.

_____

- - - - - - - - - - - -

_____

3.

_____

- - - - - - - - - - - -

_____

4.

_____

- - - - - - - - - - - -

_____

5.

_____

- - - - - - - - - - - -

_____

6.

_____

- - - - - - - - - - - -

_____

7.

_____

- - - - - - - - - - - -

_____

8.

_____

- - - - - - - - - - - -

_____

9.

_____

- - - - - - - - - - - -

_____

FOR THE TEACHER Review the picture names with children. Then have them read the words in the box. When they have completed the page, have them identify the words with *y* and the words with *ie*.

56

English-Language Learners
Time Together • Lesson 7

▶ **Circle and write the word that best completes each sentence. Cross out the other word.**

1. **my**
   by

   This is _____ bear.

2. **fry**
   tie

   He needs a new _____.

3. **cry**
   why

   Do you know _____ he needs it?

4.
   by
   fry

   Some friends are coming _____.

5.
   sky
   pie

   We will have some tea and _____.

FOR THE TEACHER Preview the page with children. Discuss each illustration, using the word it illustrates. Then have children complete the page.

58

English-Language Learners
Time Together • Lesson 7

Name _____

▶ **Write the word from the box that completes each sentence.**

| love | hello | high | opened |

1. Ty _____ the door.

2. "_____, Sly. I'm glad to see you again," said Ty.

3. "Let's fly kites up _____ in the blue sky," said Sly.

4. "I would _____ to," said Ty.

FOR THE TEACHER Talk with children about the pictures at the top of the page. Read each word and have children repeat it. Invite a volunteer to read the incomplete sentences aloud, and then have children complete the sentences.

59

English-Language Learners
Time Together • Lesson 7

▶ **Say the name of each picture. Write the word from the box that names the picture.**

fly	sky	sleepy	try	puppy

1. _____

2. _____

3. _____

4. _____

5. _____

FOR THE TEACHER Preview the page with children. Discuss each illustration, using the word it illustrates. Then have children complete the page.

60

English-Language Learners
Time Together • Lesson 7

Name _____

▶ **Cut out the names. Paste them under the pictures in alphabetical order.**

1.

2.

Deb

Meg

3.

4.

Fran

Jack

Ben

5.

6.

Ken

FOR THE TEACHER Review the alphabet with children. Write it on the board, or point it out on a classroom wall. Help children read the names, and have them point to the first letter in each. Then have children cut the names out, put them in alphabetical order, and paste them under the pictures.

61

English-Language Learners
Time Together • Lesson 7

Name _____

▶ **Circle and write the word that completes each sentence. Cross out the other word.**

1. **He's**
    He'll

    _____
    - - - - - - - - - - -
    _____ my friend.

2. **doesn't**
    wasn't

    _____
    - - - - - - - - - - -
    He _____ have

    a dog, but I do.

3. **She'll**
    Haven't

    _____
    - - - - - - - - - - -
    _____ chase

    a ball.

4. **Didn't**
    She's

    _____
    - - - - - - - - - - -
    _____ a

    good dog.

FOR THE TEACHER Discuss with children how the pictures show what the sentences mean, using the correct answer choice as you do so. Then have children complete the page.

62

English-Language Learners
Time Together • Lesson 7

Name _____

▶ **Write the word from the box that names each picture.**

| bone | dome | doze | home | hose |
| pole | robe | rope | rose | |

1.
_____
- - - - - - - -

2.
_____
- - - - - - - -

3.
_____
- - - - - - - -

4.
_____
- - - - - - - -

5.
_____
- - - - - - - -

6.
_____
- - - - - - - -

7.
_____
- - - - - - - -

8.
_____
- - - - - - - -

9.
_____
- - - - - - - -

For the Teacher Review the picture names with children. Then have them read the words in the box and complete the page.

64

English-Language Learners
Time Together • Lesson 8

▶ **Circle and write the word that answers the question or completes the sentence. Cross out the other word.**

1. Where does a king sit?

_____

- - - - - - - - - - - - -

_____

throne

grove

2. If you said something, you

_____

- - - - - - - - - - - - -

_____ .

drove

spoke

_____

- - - - - - - - - - - - -

3. He _____ a letter.

wrote

zone

4. It's part of your face.

_____

- - - - - - - - - - - - -

_____

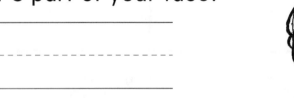

home

nose

5. You do this to a door.

_____

- - - - - - - - - - - - -

_____

close

rope

For the Teacher Talk with children about the pictures, using the correct answers. Then have children complete the page.

 66

English-Language Learners
Time Together • Lesson 8

Name _____

▶ **Write the word that completes each sentence.**

field

change

touch

twelve

1. The bee went to another _____.

2. She landed on _____ wild flowers.

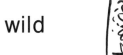

3. The flowers wait for a bee to _____ them.

4. Bees can _____ nectar into honey.

For the Teacher Talk with children about the pictures at the top of the page. Read each word and have children repeat it.

English-Language Learners
Time Together • Lesson 8

► **Circle and write the word that names the picture. Cross out the other word.**

1.
_____

joke
job

2.
_____

hope
hop

3.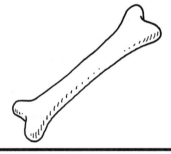
_____

bone
bond

4.
_____

rode
rod

5.
_____

pose
pot

For the Teacher Talk with children about the pictures, using the correct answer choices. Have children complete the page. When they have finished, have children practice saying all the words with the short *o* sound, and then the words with long *o*.

68

English-Language Learners
Time Together • Lesson 8

Name _____

▶ **Circle and write the word that completes the sentence. Cross out the other word.**

_____

1. The bee is _____ and yellow.

black
blast

---

2. The bees _____ out of the hive.

flag
fly

---

3. The bees find some

_____

_____ .

flames
flowers

_____

4. A _____ of sheep is near.

flock
float

For the Teacher Preview the page with children. Discuss each illustration, using the word it illustrates. Then have children complete the page.

69

English-Language Learners
Time Together • Lesson 8

Level Five

Gather Around

Name _____

▶ **Circle each picture whose name has the long i sound. Color the circled pictures.**

1.   night   2.   can

3.   fright   4.   high

5.   pin   6.   light

For the Teacher With children, read each word. Help children practice saying the words *night*, *fright*, *high*, and *light*.

▲ 3

Name _____

▶ **Circle the word that completes the sentence. Then write the word.**

_____

- - - - - - - - - - - - - - - - -

1. The bug is _____.　**go**
　　　　　　　　　　　　　　　　high

_____

- - - - - - - - - - - - - - - - -

2. Can it fly at _____?　**night**
　　　　　　　　　　　　　　　　cake

_____

- - - - - - - - - - - - - - - - -

3. Look for the _____.　**light**
　　　　　　　　　　　　　　　　right

_____

- - - - - - - - - - - - - - - - -

4. It is _____ here!　**right**
　　　　　　　　　　　　　　　take

For the Teacher Read each sentence with children and have them read the word choices. Talk about which word makes sense in each sentence. Tell children to point out *igh* in the word that makes sense. Have them complete the page.

5

English-Language Learners
Gather Around • Lesson 1

Name _____

▶ **Read the sentences. Circle and write the word that completes each sentence.**

1. The baby bird wanted to

_____

- - - - - - - - - - - - -

_____ the big birds.

join

wonder

2. The baby bird wondered if he

_____

- - - - - - - - - - - - -

could _____ to fly.

nothing

learn

_____

- - - - - - - - - - - - -

3. He _____ he could fly.

flew

thought

4. One day, he wasn't

_____

- - - - - - - - - - - - -

_____ anymore.

afraid

learn

_____

- - - - - - - - - - - - -

5. _____ could stop him as he flew.

Nothing

Wonder

For the Teacher Have volunteers read the sentence and the word choices. Discuss words children do not understand. Talk about the word that makes sense in each sentence, and have children complete the page.

6

English-Language Learners
Gather Around • Lesson 1

Name _____

▶ **Circle the word that completes each sentence. Then write the word.**

_____

- - - - - - - - - - - - - -

1. We _____ to find the right spot.

night
nose
need

_____

- - - - - - - - - - - - - -

2. It is pretty at _____.

night
dream
teeth

_____

- - - - - - - - - - - - - -

3. I feel like I can _____ the sky.

meat
reach
five

4. This hot dog is the best in

_____

- - - - - - - - - - - - - -

_____.

sight
beat
team

For the Teacher Invite volunteers to read the directions and the sentences. Talk about which word makes sense in each sentence. Have children complete the page.

7

English-Language Learners
Gather Around • Lesson 1

Name _____

▶ **Read the story. Then read the sentences
inside the raindrops. Circle the raindrop
that tells what happened in the story.**

Ann wanted to go to the lake. Rain came down.
"We can not go today," said Ann's mom. "We will
go when it is not raining."

Ann went to
the lake with
her mom.

Ann could
not go to the
lake because
of the rain.

Ann's mom
came home
late from work
one day.

For the Teacher Have a child read the story. Invite a
volunteer to read the sentence inside each raindrop.
Guide children as needed.

8

English-Language Learners
Gather Around • Lesson 1

Name _____

▶ **Read each sentence. Look at the new word in the box. Write it in the sentence.**

rake + ed

| raked |

_____

- - - - - - - - - - - - - - - - - - -

1. We _____ the yard.

chase + ing

| chasing |

_____

- - - - - - - - - - - - - - - - - - -

2. The cat was _____ the dog.

hide + ing

| hiding |

3. The dog thought he would do better

_____

- - - - - - - - - - - - - - - - - - -

_____ from the cat.

For the Teacher With children, read the sentences. Invite a volunteer to complete the first item. Remind children that the e at the end of each word is dropped before the ending is added. Guide children in completing the page.

▲
9

English-Language Learners
Gather Around • Lesson 1

Name _____

▶ **Circle the word that names each picture.**

1.

May   mat

2.

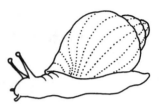

snack   snail

3.

hat   hay

4.

paint   pan

5.

pay   pet

6.

trim   train

For the Teacher Stretch the long *a* sound as you say the word with long *a* in each pair. Have children identify the letters that stand for the long *a* sound.

11

English-Language Learners
Gather Around • Lesson 2

Name _____

▶ **Look at the picture. Read the words on the mail. Write the word that completes each sentence.**

_____

- - - - - - - - - - -

1. We saw the _____.

_____

- - - - - - - - - - -

2. We ran to _____.

_____

- - - - - - - - - - -

3. We were at the farm all _____.

_____

- - - - - - - - - - -

4. It began to _____.

For the Teacher With children, read aloud each sentence. Have children read the words on the "mail." Guide them in choosing the word that makes sense in each sentence.

English-Language Learners
Gather Around • Lesson 2

▶ **Read the words in the box. Choose one word to complete each sentence.**

caught	sure	hurried

_____

- - - - - - - - - - - - - - - - - -

1. The man _____ to get near his home.

_____

- - - - - - - - - - - - - - - - - -

2. He _____ a cold.

_____

- - - - - - - - - - - - - - - - - -

3. His son made _____ he felt better.

For the Teacher With children, read the words in the box. Then have volunteers read the sentences. Make certain that children understand the words.

14

English-Language Learners
Gather Around • Lesson 2

Name _____

▶ **Read the story. Circle the words with the long sound of a̲. Write the circled words.**

Gail liked to sail. She went to the lake in May. She sailed all day with her dog.

_____

- - - - - - - - - - - - - - - - - -

_____

- - - - - - - - - - - - - - - - - -

_____

- - - - - - - - - - - - - - - - - -

_____

- - - - - - - - - - - - - - - - - -

_____

- - - - - - - - - - - - - - - - - -

_____

- - - - - - - - - - - - - - - - - -

_____

- - - - - - - - - - - - - - - - - -

_____

- - - - - - - - - - - - - - - - - -

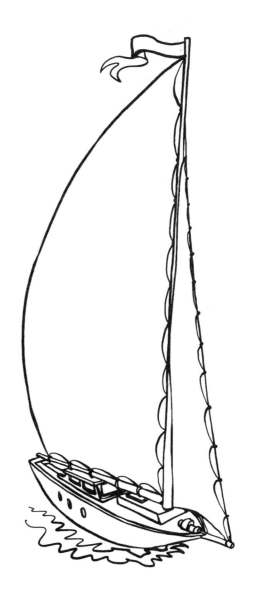

For the Teacher Invite a volunteer to read the story. With children, read the directions. Remind children to write the circled words from the story.

15

English-Language Learners
Gather Around • Lesson 2

► **Read the word and its ending above the lines. Drop the e before you add the ending. Write the word to complete the sentence.**

bake + ing

1. Are you  a cake?

like + ed

_____
- - - - - - - - - - - - - - - - - - -

2. I _____ the cake you made.

race + ed

_____
- - - - - - - - - - - - - - - - - - -

3. I _____ here to see it.

take + ing

_____
- - - - - - - - - - - - - - - - - - -

4. I am _____ some cake home.

For the Teacher With children, read the directions. Show children how the e was dropped in the first word before the ending was added. Have children complete the page.

16

English-Language Learners
Gather Around • Lesson 2

Name _____

▶ **Write the word that rhymes with the underlined word to complete each sentence.**

I. You can <u>wind</u> the toy.

feel   find

_____

- - - - - - - - - - - - - - - - - -

The baby can _____ it.

---

2. Is he <u>wild</u>?

child   flip

_____

- - - - - - - - - - - - - - - - - -

No, he's just a _____.

---

3. Let's be <u>kind</u>.

behind   away

_____

- - - - - - - - - - - - - - - - - -

Show him it's _____ him.

For the Teacher Give a few examples of rhyming words and help children read the answer choices. Discuss the illustrations, and have children complete the page.

▲18

English-Language Learners
Gather Around • Lesson 3

Name _____

▶ **Write the word that completes each sentence.**

wild

behind

find

_____
- - - - - - - - - - - - - - - - - - -

1. It is not lost. I can _____ it.

_____
- - - - - - - - - - - - - - - - - - -

2. It is not tame. It is _____ .

_____
- - - - - - - - - - - - - - - - - - -

3. It is not in front. It is _____ me.

For the Teacher Talk about the words and pictures at the top of the page. With children, read the sentences. Emphasize the word *not* as you read. Then read the directions and have children complete the page.

20

English-Language Learners
Gather Around • Lesson 3

Name _____

▶ **Write the word that completes each sentence.**

during	both	ready

_____

1. Jane and Mat got _____ to go to school.

_____

2. They _____ put on their coats.

_____

3. They had fun _____ the school day.

_____

4. At the end of the day, they were _____ to go home.

For the Teacher With children, read the directions. Have volunteers read the sentences. Point out the matching shapes at the bottom of the page. Have children complete the page.

 21

English-Language Learners
Gather Around • Lesson 3

Name _____

▶ **Write the word that completes each sentence.**

time   like

_____

- - - - - - - - - -

1. What _____ is it?

---

fire   mile

_____

- - - - - - - - - -

2. We must light the _____.

---

mind   size

_____

- - - - - - - - - -

3. Do you _____ helping with the food?

---

find   child

_____

- - - - - - - - - -

4. I can't _____ the hot dogs.

For the Teacher Preview the page with children and have them read each word choice. Help children with the meanings of unfamiliar words.

22

English-Language Learners
Gather Around • Lesson 3

Name _____

▶ **Read the selection. Find the sentence that tells the main idea. Cut it out from the bottom of the page. Paste it on the road.**

There are many kinds of bikes. Some are big. Some are small. Some are red. Some are blue. Many children like to ride bikes.

Some bikes are big.

There are many kinds of bikes.

Children have cats.

For the Teacher Read the paragraph. Invite volunteers to read the sentences with the bikes at the bottom of the page. Remind children to choose the sentence that tells what the paragraph is *mostly* about.

23

▶ **Read the sentence and the word and ending above the lines. Put together the word and ending. Double the final letter before adding the ending. Write the word to complete the sentence.**

step + ed

_____

- - - - - - - - - - - - - - - - - - -

1. He _____ onto the ladder.

slip + ed

_____

- - - - - - - - - - - - - - - - - - -

2. He _____ off of the ladder.

stop + ed

_____

- - - - - - - - - - - - - - - - - - -

3. I _____ to help him.

hop + ing

_____

- - - - - - - - - - - - - - - - - - -

4. Now we are _____.
   It's fun!

For the Teacher Read the directions with children. Talk about the word endings and their meanings. Discuss the illustrations, and have children complete the page.

24

English-Language Learners
Gather Around • Lesson 3

▶ **Read the first sentence. Write the word with the opposite meaning of the bold word to complete the sentence.**

go   ago

_____

1. We will not **stop**. We will _____.

---

soda   cold

_____

2. It is not **hot**. It is _____.

---

so   hello

_____

3. This is not **good-bye**. It is _____.

no   gold

_____

4. The answer is not **yes**. The answer is _____.

For the Teacher Discuss the meaning of the word *opposite* and give a few examples. Read aloud each sentence. Have volunteers tell which word choice is the opposite of the boldfaced word in the first sentence.

26

English-Language Learners
Gather Around • Lesson 4

Name _____

► **Cut out the word cards. Paste them to complete the sentences.**

1. Do you want to [   ]?

2. [   ], I do not!

3. I don't want to get [   ].

4. I will make you [   ] warm!

cold

No

so

go

For the Teacher Have volunteers read aloud the incomplete sentences and the words at the bottom of the page. As needed, guide children in completing the page.

English-Language Learners
Gather Around • Lesson 4

Name _____

▶ **Read the words in the box. Write the word that completes each sentence.**

pulls	floor	piece	nature

1. We want to find the surprise. We look

_____

for clues on the _____.

2. I am a good detective.

_____

I find a _____
of paper with a map.

3. We have to go to the park.

_____

He _____ the wagon.

4. There it is! We find the surprise

_____

at the _____ park.

For the Teacher With children, read the words in the box. Have volunteers read the sentences. Make certain that children understand each word. Help children determine which word makes sense in each sentence.

English-Language Learners
Gather Around • Lesson 4

▶ **Read the sentences. Write the word that completes each one.**

zone   go

_____

- - - - - - - - - - -

1. Do you want to _____ with me?

---

rose   fold

_____

- - - - - - - - - - -

2. Yes, I want to get a _____.

---

home   hope

_____

- - - - - - - - - - -

3. Let's go. We'll come _____ later.

---

ago   hold

_____

- - - - - - - - - - -

4. I'll _____ the door for you.

For the Teacher Have children read each sentence. Invite volunteers to read the word choices for each sentence. Point out the long *o* sound in each word choice. Have children complete the page.

30

English-Language Learners
Gather Around • Lesson 4

Name _____

▶ **Read the selection. Find the main idea on a pig. Paste that pig in the pen.**

Animals help on the farm. Some animals give rides. Some animals give eggs. Some animals wake us up. We like farm animals.

Some animals give eggs.

The farm is big.

Animals help on the farm.

For the Teacher Have children read the paragraph and the three sentences at the bottom of the page. Remind children to think about the main idea of the paragraph.

English-Language Learners
Gather Around • Lesson 4

Name _____

▶ **Look at the word in the box above the sentence. See how two words have been put together to make a new word. Read each sentence. Write the new word in the sentence.**

We have

| We've |

_____

- - - - - - - - - - - - - - - -

1. _____ played here before.

We would

| We'd |

_____

- - - - - - - - - - - - - - - -

2. _____ like to play here every day.

They have

| They've |

_____

- - - - - - - - - - - - - - - -

3. _____ played here, too.

They are

| They're |

_____

- - - - - - - - - - - - - - - -

4. _____ coming to play again today.

For the Teacher Have a volunteer read aloud the incomplete sentences. On the board, show children how words are combined to form contractions. Complete the first item with children.

32

English-Language Learners
Gather Around • Lesson 4

Name _____

▶ **Blend and read each word. Circle and color the picture it matches.**

1. large

2. bridge

3. edge

4. giraffe

5. gem

For the Teacher Name the three pictures in each row. Then have children read the word and circle and color the corresponding picture.

 34

English-Language Learners
Gather Around • Lesson 5

▶ **Write the word from the box that goes with each picture.**

cage	change	giant	hedge	judge	page

1. _____

2. _____

3. _____

4. _____

5. _____

6. _____

For the Teacher Review the words with children. Then have them complete the page.

36

English-Language Learners
Gather Around • Lesson 5

▶ **Write the word that completes each sentence.**

nearly   **angry**   **sorry**   **okay**

1. Celeste was _____
that she could not go out.

2. It had been raining
_____
_____ all day.

3. Celeste asked, "Would it be
_____
_____ if I went out now?"

4. "I'm _____, Celeste.
You must wait until the rain stops."

For the Teacher Talk with children about the pictures at
the top of the page. Read each word and have children
repeat it. Have volunteers read the incomplete sentences
aloud, and then have children complete the sentences.

37

English-Language Learners
Gather Around • Lesson 5

Name _____

▶ **Write the word that names the picture.**

1.    mice
           page   _____

2.    cage
           edge   _____

3.    hedge
           stage   _____

4.    dance
           space   _____

5.    badge
           page   _____

6.    strange
           judge   _____

For the Teacher Preview the page with children. Discuss each illustration, using the word it illustrates. Then have children complete the page.

38

English-Language Learners
Gather Around • Lesson 5

▶ **Look at the pictures. They tell a story. Cut
out the sentences. Paste them to show what
happens at the beginning, in the middle,
and at the end of the story.**

1. In the beginning of the story,

2. In the middle of the story,

3. At the end of the story,

they went fishing.

they left to go camping.

they set up camp.

For the Teacher Discuss the series of drawings at the top
of the page. Talk about what is happening in the story. Be
sure to use the phrases *at the beginning, in the middle,* and *at
the end.* Read the directions to children and have them
complete the page.

 39

English-Language Learners
Gather Around • Lesson 5

Name _____

▶ **Write the word from the box that completes the sentence.**

I've	she'd	They're	They've	We're

1. _____ _____ going out
in the rain.

2. _____ _____ been
splashing in the puddles.

3. _____ Cecil said, "_____
forgotten my umbrella."

4. _____ Stacy said _____
be glad to share.

5. _____ Stacy and Cecil said, "_____
good friends."

For the Teacher Preview the page with children. Discuss each contraction, making sure children know the two words it combines.

40

English-Language Learners
Gather Around • Lesson 5

Name _____

▶ **Write the word that matches the picture.**
Cross out the other word.

1. 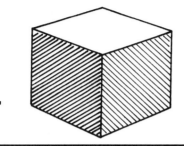 tune   cube   _____

2.  use   mule   _____

3.  cute   mule   _____

4.  rude   tune   _____

5.  tube   cute   _____

For the Teacher Preview the page with children. Discuss each
illustration, using the word it illustrates. Then read the
directions and have children complete the page.

42

English-Language Learners
Gather Around • Lesson 6

▶ **Write the word from the box that completes each sentence.**

| Excuse | use | huge | rude | perfume |

1. He needs a _____ bed.

2. "_____ me," she said. "May I help you?"

3. She used a sweet _____ _____.

4. "I don't mean to be _____ _____," he said.

5. "May I _____ this bed to test it?" he asked.

For the Teacher Go over the page with children, discussing each illustration. As you do so, use the word it illustrates. Then read the directions to the children, and have them complete the page.

44

English-Language Learners
Gather Around • Lesson 6

Name _____

▶ **Write the word that completes each sentence.**

 **brought**	 **few**	 **head**	 **read**

1. The boy _____ a flute.

2. He played a _____ tunes.

3. She _____ while he played.

4. Her _____ began to hurt.

For the Teacher Use the target words as you talk with children about the pictures at the top of the page. Read each word and have children repeat it. Invite volunteers to read the incomplete sentences aloud, and then have children complete the sentences.

English-Language Learners
Gather Around • Lesson 6

Name _____

▶ **Write the word that completes each**
sentence. Cross out the other word.

_____

- - - - - - - - - - - - - -

1. Mule and Pig gave a _____ party.

tube

huge

_____

_____

- - - - - - - - - - - - - -

2. Mule made the _____.

cake

grape

_____

_____

- - - - - - - - - - - - - -

3. Pig cut _____ of cheese.

tunes

cubes

_____

_____

- - - - - - - - - - - - - -

4. Their friends got there at _____.

hive

five

_____

_____

- - - - - - - - - - - - - -

5. They played a game with a _____.

rope

rode

_____

For the Teacher Discuss the picture with the children, using the answer choices. Then read the directions and have children complete the page.

English-Language Learners
Gather Around • Lesson 6

Name _____

▶ **Write the word that is spelled correctly.**
Cross out the other word.

1. Pig was _____ along.

skipping
skiping

2. He _____ to pick flowers.

stoped
stopped

3. He _____ over the mud.

stepped
steped

4. He _____ a flower.

dropped
droped

For the Teacher Preview the page with children. Discuss each illustration, using the word it illustrates. Then read the directions with children, and have them complete the page. ▲47

English-Language Learners
Gather Around • Lesson 6

Name _____

▶ **Write the word from the box that names each picture.**

| bread | breakfast | feather | head | meadow | thread |

1.  _____

2.  _____

3.  _____

4.  _____

5. _____

6. _____

For the Teacher Review the pictures with children, and have them read the words in the box. Then read the directions and have children complete the page.

49

English-Language Learners
Gather Around • Lesson 7

▶ **Write the word that completes the sentence. Cross out the other word.**

1. I like to _____ this sweet jelly.

spread
instead

2. I am _____ for school.

dread
ready

3. What is the _____ _____ like today?

weather
sweat

4. It is a very _____ day.

pleasant
leather

5. Take a deep _____ of the fresh air.

breath
bread

For the Teacher Preview the page with children. Discuss the illustrations, the word choices, and the incomplete sentences. Then read the directions and have children complete the page.

51

English-Language Learners
Gather Around • Lesson 7

Name _____

▶ **Write the word that completes each sentence.**

bicycle

parents

hours

carry

_____

1. Ned's _____ tuck him in.

_____

2. Ned sleeps ten _____ each night.

_____

3. Ned likes to _____ his backpack to school.

4. On Saturday afternoon, Ned

_____

rides his _____.

For the Teacher Talk with children about the pictures at the top of the page. Read each word and have children repeat it. Invite volunteers to read the incomplete sentences aloud, and then have children complete the sentences.

▲ 52

English-Language Learners
Gather Around • Lesson 7

Name _____

► **Write the word that completes each sentence. Cross out the other word.**

1. **pep**
   ten

   _____
   - - - - - - - - - - - - - - - - - - -

   Ken's pet has no _____.

2. **den**
   vet

   _____
   - - - - - - - - - - - - - - - - - - -

   The _____ looks at the hen.

3. **head**
   had

   _____
   - - - - - - - - - - - - - - - - - - -

   The feathers on her _____ look bad.

4. **bed**
   hen

   _____
   - - - - - - - - - - - - - - - - - - -

   This _____ has to get more sleep!

5. **read**
   spread

   _____
   - - - - - - - - - - - - - - - - - - -

   Ken _____ the vet's list.

For the Teacher Preview the page with children. Discuss each illustration, using the word it illustrates. Then read the directions and have children complete the page.

▲ **53**

English-Language Learners
Gather Around • Lesson 7

▶ **Cut out the sentences at the bottom of the page. Paste the sentences to tell the main idea.**

| Jen naps in a hammock. | Ben naps on the couch. | Deb naps in a chair. | Wes naps in his crib. |

| Jen likes baseball. | Ben likes to swim. | Deb is good at skating. | Wes tries to walk. |

People have different ways to exercise.

People can nap in many different places.

For the Teacher Discuss the series of drawings in each strip. Talk about what is happening. Then read the directions and have children complete the page.

54

English-Language Learners
Gather Around • Lesson 7

Phonics

Inflections:
-ed, -ing

► **Write the word that completes each sentence. Cross out the other word.**

paned
planned

1. Jed _____
   to help his mom.

_____
- - - - - - - - - - - - - - - - -
_____ _____

chopped
choped

2. Jed watched as his mom
   _____
   - - - - - - - - - - - - - - - -
   _____.

toping
topping

3. Jed put the _____
   on the pie.

_____
- - - - - - - - - - - - - - - -

hugging
huging

4. Mom is _____
   Jed.

_____
- - - - - - - - - - - - - - - -

For the Teacher Preview the page with children. Discuss each illustration, using the missing word. Then read the directions and have children complete the page.

55

English-Language Learners
Gather Around • Lesson 7

Name _____

▶ **Write the word from the box that names each picture.**

| balloon | food | goose | moon | pool | school |

1. _____

2. _____

3. _____

4. _____

5. _____

6. _____

For the Teacher Review the picture names with children,
and have them read the words in the box. Then read the
...ions and have children complete the page.

57

English-Language Learners
Gather Around • Lesson 8

Name _____

▶ **Write the word that answers the question
or completes the sentence. Cross out
the other word.**

tooth
balloon

1. What helps you eat?

_____

- - - - - - - - - - - - - - - -

_____

mood
noon

2. When do you eat lunch?

_____

- - - - - - - - - - - - - - - -

_____

shampoo
bamboo

3. What cleans your hair?

_____

- - - - - - - - - - - - - - - -

_____

igloo
boom

4. It's an ice house.

_____

- - - - - - - - - - - - - - - -

_____

boo
soon

5. This is a word to scare you.

_____

- - - - - - - - - - - - - - - -

_____

For the Teacher Preview the page with children. Discuss
each illustration, using the word it illustrates. Then read
the directions and have children complete the page.

59

English-Language Learners
Gather Around • Lesson 8

▶ **Write the word that completes each sentence.**

careful	**fire**	**shook**	**quietly**

1. Joan _____ the pot as the corn popped.

2. Her mom will keep the _____ _____ low.

3. Be very _____!

4. Joan sat _____ and leaned against her mom as they read.

For the Teacher Use the Vocabulary Words as you talk with children about the pictures in the boxes. Read each word and have children repeat it. Have volunteers read the incomplete sentences aloud, and then complete the page.

60

English-Language Learners
Gather Around • Lesson 8

▶ **Write the word that names the picture.**
Cross out the other word.

roof
tool

1. _____

tooth
toad

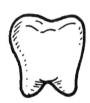

2. _____

throat
toast

3. _____

cool
tool

4. _____

soap
coat

5. _____

For the Teacher Preview the page with children. Point out each illustration, using the word it illustrates. Then read the directions and have children complete the page.

61

English-Language Learners
Gather Around • Lesson 8

Name _____

► **Read the story in the boxes. Cut out the sentences at the bottom of the page. Paste the sentences to tell what happened at the beginning, in the middle, and at the end of the story.**

Goat set the table for her friends.	Goat made some food for them.	Oh, no! Goat dropped the food!
Goat used a broom.	Goat made more food.	Goat's friends had a good time.

1. What happenend in the beginning?

┌─────────────────────────────────────┐
│   │
│   │
└─────────────────────────────────────┘

2. What happened in the middle?

┌─────────────────────────────────────┐
│   │
│   │
└─────────────────────────────────────┘

3. What happened at the end?

┌─────────────────────────────────────┐
│   │
│   │
└─────────────────────────────────────┘

┌ ─ ─ ─ ─ ─ ─ ─ ─ ─ ─ ─ ─ ─ ─ ─ ─ ─ ┐
    Goat dropped the food.
└ ─ ─ ─ ─ ─ ─ ─ ─ ─ ─ ─ ─ ─ ─ ─ ─ ─ ┘

┌ ─ ─ ─ ─ ─ ─ ─ ─ ─ ─ ─ ─ ─ ─ ─ ─ ─ ┐
    Goat's friends had a good time.
└ ─ ─ ─ ─ ─ ─ ─ ─ ─ ─ ─ ─ ─ ─ ─ ─ ─ ┘

┌ ─ ─ ─ ─ ─ ─ ─ ─ ─ ─ ─ ─ ─ ─ ─ ─ ─ ┐
    Goat set the table.
└ ─ ─ ─ ─ ─ ─ ─ ─ ─ ─ ─ ─ ─ ─ ─ ─ ─ ┘

For the Teacher Discuss the series of panels in the cartoon. Talk about what is happening in each picture. Read the directions to children and have them complete the page.

62

English-Language Learners
Gather Around • Lesson 8

Name _____

▶ **Write the word that names the picture.**
Cross out the other word.

room loom	1.		____ ------ ____
gloom broom	2.		____ ------ ____
loot boot	3.		____ ------ ____
root toot	4.		____ ------ ____
zoom groom	5.		____ ------ ____
hoot shoot	6.		____ ------ ____

For the Teacher Preview the page with children.
Discuss each illustration, using the word it illustrates.
Then read the directions and have children complete
the page.

English-Language Learners
Gather Around • Lesson 8

Answer Key

LEVEL 1 *(Guess Who)*

Page 9
Color circled pictures.

Page 11
1. cap
2. bat
3. cat
4. mat
5. map
6. pan
7. bag
8. can

Page 12
1. up
2. down
3. got

Page 13
1. cat
2. mat
3. bat
4. cap

Page 14
1. 1; 3; 2
2. 3; 2; 1

Page 15
1. hat
2. cat
3. map
4. tap
5. mat

Page 17
1. pan
2. map
3. jam
4. bat

Page 19
1. map
2. can
5. bat
6. cap
8. cat

Page 20
1. and
2. in
3. in
4. Yes
5. Oh

Page 21
1. cap
2. sand
3. bat
4. band

Page 22
1. looks
2. pats
3. comes

Page 24
Color circled pictures.

Page 26
1. bib
2. kick
3. lip
4. pig
5. six
6. sick
7. wig
8. crib

Page 27
1. walk
2. They
3. make

Page 28
1. pig
2. bib
3. wig
4. hill
5. mitt

Page 29
Paste pictures where they belong in the bottom picture.

Page 30
1. Van's
2. It's
3. That's

Page 32
Color circled pictures.

Page 34
Colored pictures:
1. tack
2. Rick
3. kick

Page 35
1. want
2. too
3. help
4. Now
5. play

Page 36
1. tack
2. sick
3. kick

Page 37
1. 2; 1; 3
2. 1; 3; 2

Page 38
1. I'll
2. You'll
3. We'll

Page 40
Color circled pictures.

Page 42
Colored pictures:
1. mop
2. box
3. dog
4. frog

Page 43
1. so
2. of
3. Don't

Page 44
Under picture of pig:
1. bib
2. lip
3. chin
Under picture of top:
1. dog
2. box
3. mop

Page 45
1. looked
2. looking
3. called
4. calling

Page 47
Paste all words on ball.

English-Language Learners
Answer Key

Page 49
1. ball
2. call
3. all

Page 50
1. Where
2. that
3. very
4. buy

Page 51
1. hill
2. mitt
3. doll
4. hall

Page 52
1. 1; 3; 2
2. 3; 1; 2
3. 2; 3; 1

Page 53
1. isn't
2. don't
3. aren't
4. Didn't

LEVEL 2 (Catch a Dream)

Page 3
1. bell-well
2. vet-wet
3. ten-pen
4. nest-vest

Page 5
1. jet
2. web
3. neck
4. hen
5. pet

Page 6
1. her
2. with
3. every

Page 7
1. jet
2. nest
3. wet
4. belt
5. net
6. bell

Page 8
1. nest
2. hill

Page 9
Circled/colored pictures:
1. spoon; spider
2. stamp; star
3. sleep; slide
4. stop; stick

Page 11
1. bath
2. them
3. path
4. thin
5. with

Page 13
1. thin
2. moth
3. cloth
4. them
5. thick

Page 14
1. could
2. use
3. new

Page 15
1. thin
2. path
3. math
4. bath
5. thick

Page 16
1. vest
2. nest
3. tent
4. dent
5. rest

Page 18
1. bug
2. bus
3. mug
4. sun
5. tub
6. cub
7. hump
8. skunk
9. rug

Page 20
1. cut-nut
2. run-sun
3. hump-bump
4. hug-bug

Page 21
1. Your
2. night
3. says

Page 22
1. hen
2. duck
3. bed
4. desk
5. jump

Page 23
1. frame
2. crab
3. grape
4. truck
5. grill
6. crown

Page 25
1. king
2. wing
3. ring
4. sing
5. swing

Page 27
1. king
2. ring
3. wing
4. sing
5. sting

Page 28
1. two
2. eat
3. from
4. gone

Page 29
1. stop
2. grass
3. skunk
4. swing
5. ring
6. bring

Page 30
1. duck
2. pig
3. eggs
4. chicks

Page 31
1. He's
2. isn't
3. He'll
4. can't
5. They'll

Page 33
1. horn
2. snore
3. stork
4. cork
5. corn

Page 35
1. snore
2. corn
3. fort
4. cord
5. fork
6. sport

Page 36
1. our
2. try
3. need

Page 37
1. for
2. torn
3. horn
4. corn
5. fort

Page 38
Circled picture:
1. bear with cup
Boxed pictures:
1. giraffe
2. fox

Page 39
1. set
2. wind
3. play
4. corn
5. pack
6. ball

Page 41
1. dish; flash
2. ship; shell
3. brush; shack
4. shorts; shelf

Page 43
1. shack
2. crash
3. splash
4. brush

5. blush
6. shell

Page 44
1. some
2. many
3. hide; away
4. Their; funny

Page 45
1. fish
2. shop
3. ship
4. dish
5. shelf

Page 46
1. The cat is big.
2. The lamp is on.

Page 47
1. trunk
2. drum
3. scarf
4. sled
5. slid

LEVEL 3 (Here and There)

Page 3
1. cheek
2. chair
3. chalk
4. cherries
5. cheese
6. beach
7. watch
8. peach

Page 5
1. chin
2. chop
3. chick
4. pitch
5. catch
6. match

Page 6
1. animals
2. around
3. fly
4. turns

Page 7
1. catch
2. fish
3. hush
4. match
5. pitch
6. hatch

Page 8
1. cl
2. fl
3. pl
4. pl
5. cl
6. pl
7. fl
8. sl
9. cl

Page 10
1. star
2. barn
3. yarn
4. cards
5. bars
6. arm
7. harp
8. cart

Page 12
1. star
2. car
3. jar
4. arm
5. dart

Page 13
1. take
2. house
3. city
4. there

Page 14
1. car
2. bars
3. cart
4. fork
5. horn

Page 15
1. barn
2. pool

Page 16
1. jumps
2. jumping
3. walking
4. walked

Page 18
1. quilt
2. queen
3. question mark
4. whale
5. wheel
6. whistle

English-Language Learners
Answer Key

Page 20
1. quilt
2. which
3. when
4. quiz
5. quack

Page 21
1. family
2. read
3. books
4. writing

Page 22
1. quick
2. quit
3. what
4. Which
5. this

Page 23
Circled picture:
1. girl with pigtails in cap
Checked pictures:
1. blonde girl in cap
2. boy in cap

Page 24
1. flag
2. clock
3. plant
4. sled
5. clip
6. plus

Page 26
1. bird
3. fern
5. shirt
6. purse
7. girl
9. fur

Page 28
1. stir
2. bird
3. curl
4. fern
5. girl

Page 29
1. way
2. four
3. full
4. find

Page 30
1. fern
2. tusk
3. pen
4. curl
5. bird
6. bus
7. vest
8. turn

Page 31
1. picture of snow falling
2. picture of school

Page 32
1. looks
2. looked
3. looking
4. finds

Page 34
1. bubble
2. bottle
3. turtle
4. needle
5. ankle
6. pickle
7. apple
8. table

Page 36
1. bubble
2. pickle
3. candle
4. turtle
5. juggle
6. rattle

Page 37
1. together
2. talk
3. place
4. school

Page 38
1. little
2. rattle
3. bottle
4. tickle

Page 39
1. smaller
2. smallest
3. faster
4. fastest

Page 41
1. road; toad
2. snow; bow
3. coat; boat
4. float; goat

Page 43
1. boat
2. snow
3. bowl
4. coat
5. road
6. goat

Page 44
1. door
2. Would
3. made
4. kind

Page 45
1. road
2. box
3. snow
4. goat
5. bowl
6. fox
7. pot
8. boat

Page 46
1. mad
2. glad
3. glad
4. sad
5. mad
6. sad

Page 47
1. called
2. talked
3. calling
4. likes

LEVEL 4 (Time Together)

Page 9
1. sleep
2. bee
3. leap
4. she
5. peach
6. eat
7. he
8. beach
9. free

Page 11
1. beads
2. beets
3. beak
4. seal
5. sleeve

Page 12
1. know
2. those
3. write
4. room

Page 13
1. read
2. teach
3. bowl
4. coach
5. beach
6. coat

Page 14
1. bird; cat; dog
2. duck; frog; hen
3. fish; goat; toad

Page 15
1. She's
2. doesn't
3. She'll
4. He's

Page 17
1. lake
2. grapes
3. caves
4. Jane
5. race

Page 19
1. snake
2. cane
3. vase
4. game
5. gate
6. cake
7. mane
8. plate
9. cape

Page 20
1. town
2. country
3. Earth
4. world

Page 21
1. cane
2. pane
3. race
4. base
5. vase

Page 22
Paste cards in correct groups.

Page 23
named; naming
raced; racing
tamed; taming
1. racing
2. tamed

Page 25
1. penny
2. sandy
3. happy
4. soapy
5. sixty

Page 27
1. puppy
2. buggy
3. happy
4. dirty
5. hilly

Page 28
1. different
2. water
3. years
4. hold

Page 29
1. party
2. yummy
3. hurry
4. thirty
5. happy

Page 30
Paste cards in correct groups.

Page 31
1. tried
2. flies
3. studied
4. cities
5. cried

Page 33
1. time
2. vine
3. dive
4. bike
5. pine
6. nine
7. hive
8. ride
9. lime

Page 35
1. hive
2. like
3. ride
4. bride
5. white

Page 36
1. cook
2. listen
3. picture
4. young

Page 37
1. kit
2. fin
3. pig
4. dime
5. bite
6. rice
7. file
8. hike
9. hit

Page 38
1. bug; mug; rug
2. clock; rock; sock
3. fan; pan; van

Page 39
1. She's
2. didn't
3. They'll
4. She'll

Page 41
1. city
2. cent
3. pencil
4. prince
5. circle
6. ice

English-Language Learners
Answer Key

Page 43
1. cereal
2. dance
3. circus
4. braces
5. dice
6. rice
7. circle
8. space
9. face

Page 44
1. almost
2. pretty
3. say
4. sound

Page 45
1. mice
2. spice
3. trace
4. price
5. space
6. lace

Page 46
1. ride
2. price
3. bride
4. rice
5. tide

Page 48
1. clown; crown
2. cow; bow
3. loud; cloud
4. sour; hour
5. shower; tower

Page 50
1. pound
2. town
3. ground
4. found
5. flowers

Page 51
1. eight
2. Dr.
3. busy
4. care

Page 52
1. trout
2. pouch
3. towel
4. scouts
5. power
6. owl

Page 53
Paste cards in correct groups.

Page 54
1. frown
2. gown
3. round
4. ground
5. clown

Page 56
1. sky
2. fly
3. cry
4. pie
5. fries
6. tie
7. why
8. shy
9. lie

Page 58
Circled word:
1. my
2. tie
3. why
4. by
5. pie
Crossed-out word:
1. by
2. fry
3. cry
4. fry
5. sky

Page 59
1. opened
2. Hello
3. high
4. love

Page 60
1. sky
2. sleepy
3. fly
4. puppy
5. try

Page 61
1. Ben
2. Deb
3. Fran
4. Jack
5. Ken
6. Meg

Page 62
1. He's
2. doesn't
3. She'll
4. She's

Page 64
1. bone
2. robe
3. rose
4. pole
5. home
6. dome
7. hose
8. rope
9. doze

Page 66
1. throne
2. spoke
3. wrote
4. nose
5. close

Page 67
1. field
2. twelve
3. touch
4. change

Page 68
Circled word:
1. joke
2. hop
3. bone
4. rod
5. pose
Crossed-out word:
1. job
2. hope
3. bond
4. rode
5. pot

Page 69
Circled word:
1. black
2. fly
3. flowers
4. flock
Crossed-out word:
1. blast
2. flag
3. flames
4. float

English-Language Learners
Answer Key

LEVEL 5 (Gather Around)

Page 3
1. night
3. fright
4. high
6. light

Page 5
1. high
2. night
3. light
4. right

Page 6
1. join
2. learn
3. thought
4. afraid
5. Nothing

Page 7
1. need
2. night
3. reach
4. sight

Page 8
1. Ann could not go to the lake because of the rain.

Page 9
1. raked
2. chasing
3. hiding

Page 11
1. May
2. snail
3. hay
4. paint
5. pay
6. train

Page 13
1. hay
2. play
3. day
4. rain

Page 14
1. hurried
2. caught
3. sure

Page 15
1. Gail
2. sail
3. lake
4. May
5. sailed
6. day

Page 16
1. baking
2. liked
3. raced
4. taking

Page 18
1. find
2. child
3. behind

Page 20
1. find
2. wild
3. behind

Page 21
1. ready
2. both
3. during
4. ready

Page 22
1. time
2. fire
3. mind
4. find

Page 23
1. There are many kinds of bikes.

Page 24
1. stepped
2. slipped
3. stopped
4. hopping

Page 26
1. go
2. cold
3. hello
4. no

Page 28
1. go
2. No
3. cold
4. so

Page 29
1. floor
2. piece
3. pulls
4. nature

Page 30
1. go
2. rose
3. home
4. hold

Page 31
1. Animals help on the farm.

Page 32
1. We've
2. We'd
3. They've
4. They're

Page 34
1. large (elephant)
2. bridge
3. edge
4. giraffe
5. gem

Page 36
1. change
2. hedge
3. judge
4. page
5. cage
6. giant

Page 37
1. angry
2. nearly
3. okay
4. sorry

Page 38
1. mice
2. cage
3. hedge
4. dance
5. badge
6. judge

Page 39
1. they left to go camping.
2. they set up camp.
3. they went fishing.

English-Language Learners
Answer Key

Page 40
1. They're
2. They've
3. I've
4. she'd
5. We're

Page 42
Written word:
1. cube
2. mule
3. cute
4. tune
5. tube
Crossed-out word:
1. tune
2. use
3. mule
4. rude
5. cute

Page 44
1. huge
2. Excuse
3. perfume
4. rude
5. use

Page 45
1. brought
2. few
3. read
4. head

Page 46
1. huge
2. cake
3. cubes
4. five
5. rope

Page 47
Written word:
1. skipping
2. stopped
3. stepped
4. dropped
Crossed-out word:
1. skiping
2. stoped
3. steped
4. droped

Page 49
1. feather
2. thread
3. head
4. bread
5. meadow
6. breakfast

Page 51
Written word:
1. spread
2. ready
3. weather
4. pleasant
5. breath
Crossed-out word:
1. instead
2. dread
3. sweat
4. leather
5. bread

Page 52
1. parents
2. hours
3. carry
4. bicycle

Page 53
1. pep
2. vet
3. head
4. hen
5. read

Page 54
1. People can nap in many different places.
2. People have different ways to exercise.

Page 55
1. planned
2. chopped
3. topping
4. hugging

Page 57
1. school
2. food
3. pool
4. balloon
5. goose
6. moon

Page 59
Written word:
1. tooth
2. noon
3. shampoo
4. igloo
5. boo
Crossed-out word:
1. balloon
2. mood
3. bamboo
4. boom
5. soon

Page 60
1. shook
2. fire
3. careful
4. quietly

Page 61
Written word:
1. roof
2. tooth
3. toast
4. tool
5. soap
Crossed-out word:
1. tool
2. toad
3. throat
4. cool
5. coat

Page 62
1. Goat set the table.
2. Goat dropped the food.
3. Goat's friends had a good time.

Page 63
Written word:
1. room
2. broom
3. boot
4. root
5. groom
6. shoot
Crossed-out word:
1. loom
2. gloom
3. loot
4. toot
5. zoom
6. hoot

English-Language Learners
Answer Key